Early Stages

THE PROFESSIONAL THEATER AND THE YOUNG ACTOR

Early Stages

THE PROFESSIONAL THEATER AND THE YOUNG ACTOR

Walter Williamson

Walker and Company
New York

First published in the United States of America
in 1986 by the Walker Publishing Company, Inc.

Published simultaneously in Canada by John Wiley & Sons,
Canada, Limited, Rexdale, Ontario.

Library of Congress Cataloging-in-Publication Data

Williamson, Walter.
  Early stages.

  Includes index.
  Summary: Presents a brief history of the theatre and
describes the necessary qualities, training, and
experience needed by prospective actors and actresses,
as well as various opportunities in the acting profession. Also profiles ten young performers describing
the development of their careers.
    1. Acting—Vocational guidance—Juvenile
literature.   2. Children as actors—United States—
Juvenile literature.   3. Theater—Juvenile literature.
[1. Acting—Vocational guidance.   2. Vocational
guidance.   3. Actors and actresses]   I. Title.

PN2055.W55   1986   792'.028'02373   85-26467
ISBN 0-8027-6624-2
ISBN 0-8027-6630-7 (reinforced)

Book design by Teresa M. Carboni

Printed in the United States of America

10 9 8 7 6 5 4 3 2 1

This book is dedicated to

Frances Joyner Kitchen, who taught me to love theater,

Robert Porterfield, who taught me to respect theater as a business,

Robroy Farquhar, who taught me to respect the people in the theater, and

Robert John Versteeg, who taught me to love the art in myself more than myself in the art,

and to Sam, who let it all happen.

ACKNOWLEDGMENTS

Many people become part of a book as it grows from an idea to a bound volume. Some of them are mentioned in the text. But many are not. Carol Anderson got the whole thing going by sending me to Beth Walker, and I thank them both. The staff at Solters/Roskin/Friedman, in particular Susan Lee and Keith Sherman, helped with two important pieces, as did the American Theater Wing, by providing transcripts of their Matthew Broderick interview. Mark Sumner of the Institute of Outdoor Drama, Chapel Hill, N.C., and Margaret Harper of *Texas* helped greatly. Susan McNeill took more messages than anyone should have to, and Christa Storey was a valuable mirror. To the many friends who got tired of reading drafts but smiled and read anyway, my thanks.

Contents

Introduction

The actor stands in the darkened area just behind the heavy red velvet curtain. His costume of silk and fur falls gracefully around him. Behind him in the shadows other actors, stage managers, and property people whisper and scurry around, attending to their last-minute tasks before the play begins. Beyond the curtain several hundred people chatter excitedly as they settle into their seats. Behind the actor is a world made of lights and costumes, scenery and makeup. In front of him, on the other side of the curtain, the audience belongs to the "real" world. Once the curtain goes up, once the play begins, it will be the actor's job to draw that audience out of everyday existence into the temporary reality of the stage. The actor is the entrance point through which the audience passes for a brief visit to a world of imagination and make-believe.

At the edge of the curtain the actor sees the reflection of the house lights as they begin to dim. The sound coming from the audience changes and starts to subside. Quickly he looks around to make sure the chair he must sit in is in the right position. His hand comes up to satisfy himself that his wig is on tight. He runs through the first few words of the first line he must speak. Music begins, and the narrow strip of house light visible at the edge of the curtain fades to black. Behind him the hushed voice of a stage manager whispers "Curtain up—*go!*" In the dark he hears the whirring of ropes passing through pulleys and feels the air and sound in front of him expand as the velvet barrier between him and the audience moves away.

The audience has become quiet. Now the music comes to an end and the stage lights come up full. There the actor stands, with hundreds of eyes on him, waiting to be led into the world of the play. The actor will be the tour guide. He speaks and the play has begun.

Is this a professional production in a New York theater where the audience has paid as much as fifty dollars for each ticket? Is this a school assembly program with a student audience as excited about getting out of class for an hour as they are about getting to watch a play? It could be either. The sequence of events, the activities and concerns of the people involved, and the job at hand—drawing the audience into the world of the play—are the same whether the actor gets a paycheck at the end of the week or is merely congratulated (or teased) as he walks down the hall on the way to his next class. Obviously there is a big difference between the levels of skill required for a school play and for a Broadway production, just as there are different levels of skill required for touch football and for the Super Bowl. But the rules of both the games and the productions are essentially the same, and just as most professional football players began by playing backyard ball, so must professional actors began their careers in school and community plays.

Professional theater, however, offers an opportunity that professional sports do not. The demands of weight, experience, and agility limit participation in professional football to those with a physical maturity that comes only with age. On the other hand, there are a great many professional opportunities every year for actors described in casting notices as "young adults," "teens," and even "children." In recent years some of the biggest Broadway productions, including *Annie, The King and I,* and *Porgy and Bess,* have employed dozens of children. In nonmusical plays such as *Brighton Beach Memoirs, The Corn Is Green,* and *Joe Egg,* teenagers are cast in roles that require them to display both their natural youth and a high degree of acting skill. In regional professional theater the most frequently staged play in recent years has been *A Christmas Carol,* and directors from Maine to California are constantly on the lookout for kids who can play Tiny Tim. These are serious commercial productions, and the young people involved are treated as professional actors and paid standard professional wages for their work.

Ralph Carter was not yet ten years old and singing a leading role in the Broadway musical *Raisin* when he was tapped to play the younger brother in the popular television series *Good Times.* When seventeen-year-old Liza Minnelli appeared off-Broadway in *Best Foot Forward* in 1963, she was considered a talented newcomer. A young man named Burt Reynolds had impressed Broadway audiences in *Look: We've Come Through* a couple of years before. More recently Sean Penn and Kevin Bacon appeared together off-Broadway in *Slab Boys* (1983) before films like *The Falcon and the Snowman* and *Footloose* brought them to a wider public. Hollywood star Carol Burnett was a New York unknown just into her twenties before *Once Upon a Mattress* brought her to the attention of the media. Rock singer Meatloaf began his stage career as a teenage actor in an off-Broadway play. The thing all these successful professionals have in common is the fact that they started early and on the stage. They understood that the lessons they would learn dealing with a live audience night after night would strengthen their talent and aid their ability to perform in whatever medium they chose. Many return to the stage between film, television, and recording engagements. They know that the stage is the basis for all performing styles and will continue to give shape and refinement to their craft.

The stories in this book are about young people who have had the opportunity to become professionals or who are studying to become professional actors on the stage. In order to understand more about them and the lives they lead, it is important to first understand a bit about how theater works and how young people fit into the theatrical industry.

Over the centuries acting has developed into an art form with its own skills and disciplines. Some of these skills can be studied and improved. Some are dependent upon natural talent.

An actor must be able to speak and move well so that people can see and hear the character clearly. These movement and speech skills can be enhanced by studying singing and dancing. In order to understand how characters in early times behaved, what their attitudes were, and how they saw themselves, an actor must study history. Most actors read a great many biographies to learn how events in people's lives can effect the way they think and act. To gain experience, the young actor may work in school or religious drama, or in community theater with other youths or with local adults. With each role the beginning thespian plays, his or her experience grows and the use of voice, movement, and character motivation becomes easier.

In addition to vocal, movement, and emotional skills, one more element must be present. It is a natural talent shared with teachers, politicians, and preachers, and it is referred to as *stage presence*. It is an ability to capture the attention of an audience and hold it. It is a kind of magnetism that has little to do with whether or not the individual is personable and outgoing offstage. Rather, it has to do with an ability to share one's energy, focus, and spirit with an audience. Without this gift no one can sustain a professional stage career for long.

Acting can be an enjoyable and rewarding hobby, and many young people and adults all over the country are delighted to study and practice the craft on an amateur basis for the sheer joy of the work. Others, however, are driven toward a more complete involvement. For them, nothing will do but a full-time professional career. It is not that they *want* to be in theater—it is that they *must* be in theater. Most responsible teachers discourage students from pursuing theater as a profession. The opportunities are severely limited and the chances for success are very small. At any given time only about ten percent of the professional actors in America are working. This compares with more than ninety percent of the general population. Most actors need a second occupation in order to support themselves.

Once the decision has been made to aim for theater as a profession, the options become a bit more complex. Many towns have teachers of dance, music, and even drama who will begin lessons as early as age three. These classes, usually available after school, are good for both the enthusiastic amateur and the budding professional. There are also some specialized high schools, where students with exceptional talent can spend part of their day in regular classes and part in artistic training. New York's High School of Performing Arts, which was the basis for the film and television show *Fame,* is one example of such a school.

After high school the student of theater may choose to

go directly into competiton for theater jobs. Another plan would take the student to a college with a strong theater department. Yet another approach would include attending one of many professional training conservatories around the country. The Neighborhood Playhouse and the American Academy of Dramatic Art, both in New York, are among the best-known examples of this kind of school. Here the emphasis is limited to theater training, and no academics are taught. However, graduation from such schools does not include a standard degree, and the usefulness of the education may be limited if the student later decides to work outside the profession.

After formal training, the truly professional part of the actor's career begins. This is when the performer actually starts to look for a job. Some actors work through agents. Others do not. Usually, beginning actors don't need the services of an agent. Smaller roles are generally cast from open auditions that anyone can attend. It is not until the actor begins to build a reputation and needs someone to sort out conflicting jobs, advise on career moves, and negotiate higher salaries that the agent becomes a useful associate.

Except for the very few who become "stars" and are offered more work than they can handle, the process of looking for work is much the same whether the actor is a young beginner or an experienced adult. A producer (who is the money and business person in the process) decides to present a play. He hires a director. The director announces in weekly trade newspapers that auditions will be held at a certain time and that roles being cast will include certain types. Hundreds of actors are then interviewed by the director and his or her assistants. Eventually these hundreds are narrowed down to just a few candidates for each role.

At that point casting has less to do with talent and

experience and more to do with the basic look and personality of the actors involved. For instance, if the characters being cast include a family, and the actors who will play the parents are both tall, thin, and fair-skinned, it is unlikely that a director would cast an actress who is short, thick, and dark as their teenage daughter.

Once the casting process has been completed and the actors for the play selected, they are signed to contracts under regulations established by Actors' Equity Association, the actors' union. Actors' Equity determines rules under which professional productions rehearse and perform—how many hours the actors may work each day, what safety measures must be taken for their protection, minimum salaries for actors and stage managers, and so forth. These minimum salaries are just that: minimums. "Name" or "star" actors may negotiate much higher salaries.

A stage production may come under any one of several types of Actors' Equity contract:

- *Theater for Young Audiences* (TYA) governs tours to schools and communities for student audiences.

- *Stock* theaters are most active in the summer in tourist areas. They usually produce musicals and light comedies as entertainment for people on vacation.

- *Regional repertory* theaters such as the Arena Stage in Washington, D.C., and the American Conservatory Theater in San Francisco are companies that concentrate on more serious theater and are likely to do Shakespeare and other classic plays.

- *Dinner theaters* combine dining with a play and tend to focus on entertainment rather than on literary or social themes.

- *Production tours* are major commercial ventures either going to or coming from New York. Most Broadway musical successes go on tour. The cast will usually be headed by a star. These tours are booked into large civic auditoriums and concert halls.

In recent years there has been a decline in the number of productions presented in New York. Therefore there is now more work outside the city than on Broadway and off-Broadway. Yet these New York shows are the flagship productions of professional theater. For audiences and actors the idea of seeing or being in a Broadway play holds a magic all its own.

The term *Broadway* simply means a New York theater in which the number of seats in the audience—and therefore the potential for making money from selling tickets—is large enough that Actors' Equity requires its highest minimum salary for actors working on that stage. There are only about thirty-five theaters clustered around Times Square in New York that meet this definition. For off-Broadway the seats are fewer, so the potential revenue is smaller and the required salaries are lower. Off-Broadway theaters are found all over New York, although most are in Greenwich Village.

Outside New York the union allows some roles to be played by actors who are not union members. This enables young persons to enter the profession at any one of several levels. A child living near a summer stock theater might be cast as one of the little girls in *Annie*. Or a local teenager might be asked to play young Siward in a regional repertory production of *Macbeth*.

In New York most of the work is governed by the union, and the level of talent and experience is very high. The level of competition is high too. Just like adult performers, young performers may spend a lot more time *looking* for work than actually performing a role in a play. The cost of lessons in music, dance, and acting is very great. Photographs must be printed and sent to dozens of producers and directors. Most actors assume they will fail at twenty to thirty auditions for every one job they actually get. And once they get a job, the play may run only a few weeks. Then the actor finds himself starting all over again.

The rewards, on the other hand, can be great. Sometimes young actors make more money than their parents. Young people who become "stars" are photographed, interviewed, and advertised all over the world. People want to meet them. They are invited to fancy parties, stay in fine hotels, and meet other famous people.

Beyond the glamour, however, is the fact that young actors share the same experience that has inspired and motivated all actors from the time of the story-telling caveman to the boy or girl performing tonight on Broadway. It is an experience of sharing something with a living, breathing audience. It is saying a line or singing a song or finishing a dance and hearing the audience sob or laugh or applaud. It is knowing that something *you* did captured the attention and touched the emotions of those hundreds of people sitting out in the dark. It is a special feeling. It happens only between a living performer and a living audience. It is a unique kind of communication—one that young people can be part of.

1

Robert McNeill

A JOURNEY TO BROADWAY

It was early autumn, but the days were still warm. Not until evening did the cool of approaching winter fill the New York streets and cause people to button their buttons and step a little quicker. It was early evening now. Times Square was a jumble of traffic. Cabs and cars and buses filled the streets as people filled the sidewalks. Some had worked late and were just now on their way home. Most were on their way to the theater.

Robby McNeill stepped off the bus at the corner of Forty-seventh Street and Broadway on the west side of Times Square. He looked up at the huge animated clock ten stories high on the far side of the street. Seven twenty-six P.M. *Good,* thought Robby, *I won't be late after all.* Four minutes was more than enough to walk the half block to work. As he passed under the marquee of the Lunt-Fontanne Theatre, he glanced up at the poster. The bold print announced Cicely Tyson in *The Corn Is Green.* Lower on the poster, in a long list of names in smaller print, he would find Robert McNeill listed among the other actors. After all these weeks it still gave him a thrill.

Robby turned in at a black door marked STAGE ENTRANCE. He was required by union rules to be in the

Robert McNeill first performed in public as a magician. He developed a regional reputation as an entertainer before expanding his performing talent into acting.

theater by 7:30, half an hour before curtain time. He looked quickly at the doorman's clock. Seven twenty-nine. *Made it,* he thought. As he signed in on the sheet on the call board, an assistant stage manager touched his arm and said, "There's a meeting onstage, right now!" Quickly Robby made his way through the passage, past the prop table, past Miss Tyson's dressing room, and into the area behind the set. All of the cast were assembled and all of them were looking at him. Robby had a sinking feeling that he had done something very wrong. What could it be? He was playing only a very small part.

A representative from the union, Actors' Equity, quickly explained that the show was running out of money. If every member of the cast agreed to a cut in pay, the show could stay open another few weeks. But it had to be everyone. If anyone objected, the play would close tonight. Every other actor in the cast had agreed to the cut. Robby was the only person left. If he agreed to the cut, the play would stay open. If he didn't, the play would close.

This was a major Broadway production. Cicely Tyson was an international star known both for her work on the stage and as the leading actress in such films as *Sounder* and *The Autobiography of Miss Jane Pittman*. The cast was filled with faces that could be instantly recognized from films and television. Hollywood star Elizabeth Taylor was one of the producers. The production had cost nearly a million dollars to put together. And now at this moment Robby McNeill, from a small town in North Carolina, twenty-two years old and only a year out of college, was responsible for the whole show.

Robert McNeill has the kind of clean-cut, cheerful, open good looks that will make people think of him as "boyish" well into his adulthood. He smiles easily and frequently. There is nothing exotic or mysterious about his appearance or his manner. It is a surprise, then, to hear that his first public performance was as a magician.

Robby was born and grew up in Fayetteville, a small city in North Carolina. Fayetteville is the hometown for Fort Bragg, the largest U.S. military installation in the world. Because of the military climate, Fayetteville tends to change more rapidly and frequently than many towns. Soldiers and their families constantly come and go. But Robby's childhood was secure and stable. His father is a businessman and his mother recently retired after a career as a schoolteacher and educational administrator.

Perhaps because of the unsettling influence of the army base, Rob and Doris made a specific effort to give Robby and his older sister, Libby, the advantages of

At sixteen Robby was entertaining at children's parties and company picnics. Here he does his magic act for a community Christmas party.

their prosperity and their deeply felt religious and social values. There were music lessons and vacations to interesting places. There were family outings and trips to concerts and cultural events. Somehow, out of this solidly middle-class environment, Robby developed as a showman. When asked where the desire to perform came from, Robby says, "I don't know. It's not the kind of thing you decide on. It's just *there,* and one day you realize that it's been there all along."

"All along" began in kindergarten. Robby remembers being cast as Papa Bear in *Goldilocks.* He was well-rehearsed in the role, but when the costumes arrived, the Papa Bear suit was much too large for his young frame. So Robby was reassigned a lesser role and a bigger boy was given the costume and the choice part.

Robby soothed his thwarted theatrical ambition with puppet shows. He built puppets and puppet stages in his back yard, and when he ran out of audiences in the neighborhood, his sister and the family housekeeper would sometimes come and watch.

From puppets his interest shifted to ventriloquism. His parents helped him get a real dummy to sit on his knee. Today he remembers that the dummy could say things that he could not. Robby was often surprised when the dummy, Danny O'Day, would come up with a snappy bit of conversation or a wisecrack. Something inside Robby was trying to get out, and it found its release in the patter he fed through the dummy's mouth.

The puppet performances and the ventriloquism were for family and friends. So was the magic act—at first. But at age twelve, with several years of practicing his tricks at the dinner table behind him, he saw an ad in the local paper. The county fair was looking for variety acts. Without telling anyone he called and made an appointment. Only then did he ask his mother to drive him to the audition. She was completely surprised. Then she sighed her indulgent sigh and got out her car keys. "Robby does what Robby wants to do," says Doris McNeill. "Somehow he always finds a way."

A twelve-year-old doing a polished magic act became the hit of the county fair that year, and for the first time in his life Robby was paid for performing. A lot of people saw those performances, and soon Robby was being hired to perform for birthday parties and company picnics all over the Fayetteville area.

It was a junior high drama teacher who first helped Robby translate his ability to perform in front of an audience into an ability to portray characters in plays. By now he had developed an ease onstage that made acting a natural next step. From biographies and "how-to" books about magic and magicians, his reading list began to expand to include actors and acting and plays and theater history.

By the time he went to high school, Robby was fully committed to the theater as a career. When he wasn't in class he was in rehearsal, and at night he was torn between doing his algebra assignment and studying his lines for his next role. In addition to the plays done in school, Fayetteville had a youth theater for student performers. There was also the Fayetteville Little Theater and the Fort Bragg Playhouse. During his junior year he became part of a group of students selected from area high schools who toured with a musical review all over the state.

Everyone in Fayetteville knew Robby was talented. But the idea of theater as a profession was so foreign to most of them that it was hard to relate to Robby as a future actor. That made the few people who did understand and encourage him much more special.

In a way the decision of what to do after high school was made for him. Every year the North Carolina School of the Arts gives one—and only one—full scholarship. The school was founded by then Governor Terry Sanford. The award is named in his honor. Hundreds of students across North Carolina audition for the scholarship as thousands of students apply for regular admission to the school. In its twenty-year history, NCSA has gained an international reputation for excellence in performer training. Larger, older, richer schools envy the seriousness of purpose and the consistently high quality of the graduates.

In 1978 the Terry Sanford Scholar at the North Carolina School of the Arts was Robert McNeill.

NCSA was a major step for Robby. No longer was he the most talented kid in town. Now he was one talented kid in a whole school of talented kids. He studied fencing, makeup, dance, and music. He studied acting with teachers whose standards were based on the best

16

The Star Spangled Girl *was one of Robby's first leading roles in a nonmusical play. The part required more than just entertaining, and was a valuable step in his development.*

theater art. He continued to practice his magic, and added juggling and mime to his bag of tricks.

During summer vacations he performed his variety acts at resorts in Virginia and South Carolina. Now the audiences were strangers, not hometown people with familiar faces. But the strangers liked him too. Robby's skill and experience expanded and matured. By the spring of 1982, with graduation just around the corner, he was ready to step out into the arena of full-time professional theater.

The North Carolina School of the Arts belongs to a group of colleges known as the League of Theatre Training Programs. Every spring the league invites major talent agents and casting directors to Lincoln Center in New York, where the graduating seniors of the various schools perform for people who can help

17

them find work. At the league auditions in 1982, members of the J. Michael Bloom agency saw Robby perform a scene and immediately asked him to sign a contract so they could represent him. They would give him professional advice, send him on auditions, and negotiate contracts for him. Robby signed with the Bloom agency that same week.

The first week he was in New York the agency sent Robby out on three auditions. Although he didn't get work right away, the agency continued to be impressed with both his talent and his professionalism. Many actors wait on tables in restaurants between acting jobs in order to pay the bills. Others take temporary office work. Robby had another way to make survival money.

Street performers are a colorful part of life in New York. On one corner you might find a guitar player singing country songs while down the block a brass trio might be piping out Bach. Tumblers and dancers and mimes and jugglers space themselves through the parks and around the major museums. Each does his or her act and then passes a hat to collect coins and bills from the amused onlookers. Robby found space in front of the Metropolitian Museum of Art. Sometimes he would juggle. Sometimes he would do pantomime pieces. Sometimes he would do magic tricks. Sometimes he would do all three.

Street performing paid him better than he expected and gave him the flexibility to perform *what* he wanted *when* he wanted. A good day might bring one hundred dollars or more. This gave him the resources to learn more about New York. He went to plays and movies, stores and museums. He explored the subway system and attended open air concerts in Central Park.

The agency continued to send him on auditions, but nothing really connected until mid-winter, when a candy-bar commercial became his first paid job in the city. That and meeting a girl named Susie, were the best things that could be said for his first New York winter.

One cold February night about midnight Robby's phone rang. It was Walter, a friend from North Carolina also transplanted to New York.

"Robby, I just heard that Vivian Matalon, the director, is holding some private auditions this week for *The Corn Is Green*. The play doesn't go into rehearsal for months, but Matalon is going to be in Europe directing a movie until right before the rehearsals start. You really should audition for the role of Morgan Evans. You'd be perfect. Call your agent first thing in the morning and make them get you an audition."

Marilyn, Robby's agent, was skeptical at first. The play wasn't scheduled to open until June. But she agreed to call. To Marilyn's surprise, Mr. Matalon agreed to see Robby in two days. Robby called Walter. "I've never even read *The Corn Is Green*. Help!" Walter called a dialect coach he knew so that Robby could get an emergency crash course in the thick Welsh accent that most of the characters speak in. Robby read the play again and again, concentrating on the scenes with Morgan Evans, the leading male role. Again and again he spoke the words in the unfamiliar dialect. His mouth was sore from making the strange sounds. Carefully he planned what he would wear, choosing a shirt and slacks that would suggest the rough homespun tweeds of the Welsh coalminers without looking like a costume. The forty-eight hours were very busy.

Finally the day and hour arrived and Robby was ushered into a studio and introduced to Mr. Matalon. The stage manager, a young man, got up to read the lines of the elderly woman with whom Morgan plays most of his scenes. Robby took a deep breath and began.

The whole audition was over in just a few minutes. "If we don't decide to use you as Morgan," Mr. Matalon was suddenly saying in his soft British accent, "would you be willing to play one of the smaller parts?"

For a split-second Robby's mind flashed back to kindergarten. Somewhere a voice was saying, "If he can't wear the Papa Bear costume, then he can play one of the smaller parts." With only that tiny hesitation Robby said, "Yes, of course." He got one of the smaller parts.

In May it started. There was the first day of rehearsal with a cast filled with famous faces. For a month Robby was in the studio almost every day learning movement and lines and songs with the other actors. There were costume fittings and photo sessions. There were classes with a dialect coach and consultations with the makeup designer. In June the whole company moved to Washington, D.C., and Robby moved into a hotel. Final rehearsals were at the Kennedy Center, where the play tried out for eight weeks. Then back to New York for two more weeks of previews before the formal opening. On August 22, 1983, *The Corn Is Green* opened on Broadway with Robert McNeill playing one of the small parts. The opening night audience was filled with celebrities, and dozens of cameras flashed every time a limousine pulled to the curb outside the theater. Inside, among the critics and bejeweled first-nighters, Walter, who helped the whole thing get started sat with his wife across the aisle from Elizabeth Taylor. Robby's girlfriend, Susie, sat with them. Having opened once in Washington and having previewed for the past two weeks, Robby felt strangely calm on this opening night. Most of the important critics had seen the show during previews. Now the actors could simply play the play. For Robby it was a relief. He felt like a professional doing a job he had been trained to do.

Susie went with Robby to the opening night party at the Copacabana. Everyone at the party was anxious. The production had not been what many in the company had hoped for, and when the newspaper reviews were brought in, they were highly critical. Not one of the major critics really liked the show, and everyone at the party realized that they would soon be out of work. The party broke up early and one older actor patted Robby on the hand and said, "Well, kid, welcome to show biz."

Robby and Susie walked slowly along the edge of Central Park. The night air was warm, and as they neared the Plaza hotel the unmistakable scent of horses reached them. For years in movies and television shows set in New York they had seen pictures of the elegant hansom cabs that can be rented in front of the Plaza for drives through the park. Robby in his tuxedo turned to Susie in her soft pink gown. "We had better make the most of this night. It looks like there won't be any more of these for a while." They rode through Central Park at midnight in a hansom drawn by a high-stepping horse. But they were also drawn by a sense of good humor and a graceful acceptance of what the theater is really like. Some plays are hits, and run for years. Most do not. Robby had played his role well and he knew he really had nothing to feel bad about.

It was a few nights later that the Actors' Equity representative placed the burden of possibly closing the show on Robby's shoulders. He agreed, of course, to the pay cut, and the play ran for a few more weeks. But the bad reviews had hurt and the audiences remained small. *The Corn Is Green* closed in late September.

Robby has remained in New York. He has done several plays and commercials and continues to audition for more work and better roles. The commercials pay well and he occasionally does his street act. In 1984

Robby uses this picture for professional purposes today. His agent sends it out whenever there is a role he might be right for.

he and Susie were married. She continues to work as a researcher for *The New York Times*, and between them they provide for a comfortable life.

When Robby remembers his first exposure to professional actors, he thinks back to guest performers who came to Fayetteville when he was younger. "They had a way of speaking, of moving, that was . . . well . . . different. Special. They seemed to know how to make their voices say more than the words." Today Robby is special too. There is a confidence in his speech and in the way he moves. He knows what life he has chosen and who he is, and when anyone asks him what he does for a living, there is neither pride nor hesitation when he says simply, "I'm an actor."

AUTHOR'S NOTE: The American Theater Association publishes an annual directory of theaters, both commercial and educational throughout the country. Many libraries stock this book. For further information, the association address is listed in Appendix D.

2

Holly Taylor

SUMMER STOCK IN THE BLOOD

Morning comes with heavy mist in the low mountains of western North Carolina. It gathers in the night among the thick pines and poplars and at first light starts a slow rise to meet the sun. As if waking from sleep, the moisture hangs in the early air, reluctant to travel, still tired from a too-short night. From a distance this morning haze gives the place a distinctive color, and the early English who settled here spoke of the blue ridges of the area. The name held, and today the entire range that runs from the Shenandoah in Virginia down to meet the Great Smokies that straddle the Tennessee-North Carolina border is known as the Blue Ridge Mountains.

Summers here are cool and fragrant, with the aroma of the forest that blankets the terrain. During the nineteenth century wealthy families from Charleston, eager to escape the heat and humidity and stench of the urban coast, built summer homes in the area around a great open slab of granite some thirty miles south of Asheville. The formation, nearly an acre in size, had been an Indian landmark for centuries, and as the village of "Flat Rock" grew, the rock itself became the centerpiece of the community.

In the 1940s a troupe of actors from New York led by an expatriate Englishman with the unlikely name of Robroy Farquhar set up a tent at the edge of the rock and presented a series of plays. Audiences arrived from summer communities around the region and from Asheville to the north and Spartanburg, S.C., to the south. The response was good and the troupe kept coming back. After a few seasons they built a wooden stage that opened onto the tent where the audience sat. Later they built a barnlike shelter over the audience. Eventually they built a fully equipped stage house and dormitories and a dining hall. By the time Robroy died in 1983, the Flat Rock Playhouse was a thriving company involved in year-round touring educational programs in addition to the ten-week summer theater season, and the artistic service rendered to the area and to the region had won it the designation "State Theater of North Carolina."

"Robby," as he was universally known, would be proud that the playhouse is continuing to grow under the leadership of his son, Robin. Like his father, Robin is a gentle person, totally dedicated to the theater. And he is both sensitive and responsive to the expectations and tastes of the audience the playhouse serves. Most of the selections presented are light in nature, with a leaning to comedies and mysteries. Robin understands, as his father did before him, that summer audiences are not generally interested in tragically profound drama or heavy social commentary. Yet the company has distinguished itself for fifteen years with its annual production of *Look Homeward, Angel,* based on the Thomas Wolfe novel set in nearby Asheville. And actors who work at Flat Rock appreciate the fact that in every season there is one play of more serious consequence that the management seems to feel is important whether the audiences take to it or not. Between the

Neil Simons and John Patricks there will be an *A Man for All Seasons* or an *A Cry of Players*. "Robby" used to say, "This one is for the actors."

Flat Rock is not unique among summer stock companies. Across the country dozens of such companies operate every summer. Some play a season or two in a resort location and then are gone. Some, like Flat Rock, last for many years and become part of the areas they serve. And each is special to both its audience and to the performers who know it as a summer home or as a launching pad for a professional career.

The regular day at Flat Rock starts at 10:00 A.M., according to Actors' Equity regulations, with rehearsal for the next week's show. Some of the apprentices will be in this rehearsal either as performers of small roles or as assistants to the stage manager, the director, or the props master. Others will be working in the costume and scenery shops behind the stage. Still others will be out in town collecting props or distributing posters with the promotion director. The assignments are rotated from week to week so that everyone has a chance to work in every area. While all this is going on, there is a grounds staff at work keeping the property in order, a household staff providing meals and doing laundry, and an office staff running the business and operating the box office. Flat Rock Playhouse is now a nonprofit corporation, and all of this activity takes place under the authority of a voluntary board of directors made up of interested citizens from all over the area.

Into this environment has come during this summer of 1985 one Holly Taylor. She has the credentials to be a person of some importance in this company. They include her father's reputation as a regional celebrity in radio and television, and a striking look enhanced by dark hair and eyes, an asset on any stage. "A cherry tree in full bloom," was the description one admiring observer gave, adding, "sparkling and warm and lovely." Most of all, Holly Taylor has a family inheritance that gives her claim to a position at Flat Rock. Holly is the granddaughter of Robroy Farquhar, the founder of the theater, and niece of Robin Farquhar, the current managing director. Her grandmother, Leona, lives on the property, and Holly has been a regular visitor for as long as she can remember. It would be easy to understand how Holly could feel entitled to be part of the company. By birth, by history, by connections, she, in some ways, *belongs* at Flat Rock. And what has all this background gained her in the social and artistic structure of the theater community? "Nothing!" says Holly. "And I wouldn't want it any other way."

Holly has entered the company as an apprentice and will make her way up by hard work if she will do it and talent if she has it. "Uncle Robin sat me down when I first got here and told me not to expect any favors. I told him I didn't want any. And I haven't gotten any. If anything, I have had to work harder than the others to prove I wasn't getting anything extra." That goes with the family tradition. Summer theater is hard work. In less than fifty hours of rehearsal time, an entire play must be mounted each week of the season. Scenery, costumes, and lights must be built, set up overnight, and taken down a few days later almost before the paint is dry. Promotion efforts must be enormous to gather an audience for just seven performances of a given production. And the process is repeated eight or more times every summer. Everyone works hard. No one works harder than the people at the top. Holly's memories of her grandfather involve running after him as he hurried from office to theater to shop on errands. Thousands of details must be seen to, and Holly came to Flat Rock

On summer visits to Flat Rock as a preteen, Holly was a charmer. Her warm sense of humor shows in this early picture.

this summer fully aware of the intensity of the job to be done. Her uncle Robin has maintained the same work pattern as his father, and it is not at all unusual to see the office lights burning deep into the night after everyone else has gone to bed.

The only concession to her family connection is the fact that Holly is living at her grandmother's house. "I wanted to live in the dorm with everyone else. But Grandmother put her foot down." When Leona puts her foot down, everyone pays attention. Not at all a typical grandmotherly type, Leona Farquhar is a force to be reckoned with. Slim and active, vivacious and dynamic, she runs a health food store and serves as the best evidence of the value of her products. At the theater she is a mother hen to the company, a taskmaster to the household staff, and a lovely and charming hostess for Playhouse social events. Robroy and Leona divorced many years ago but remained good friends, co-parents, and helpmates through the rest of Robby's life.

Holly's home is in Key West, Florida. That's where her parents live. Dick and Keats (Farquhar) Taylor met and married in Charlotte, N.C. Dick brought two sons to

the marriage and Keats brought one. When Holly was born she was their first child, but she already had three older brothers.

Dick had acted on the stage in his early career, but turned to television and radio and became something of a local star with a large personal following in the Charlotte market. Holly has inherited some of the mellowness of his rich resonant voice as she has inherited her dark hair and sparkling deep eyes from her mother. Keats had done some early acting, too, more as part of the family tradition at Flat Rock than as a vocational desire. She found her real art form in painting. Holly got used to people saying "You're Dick Taylor's girl?" as if that made her special. At home he was just her father, Holly says, "But every now and then he comes out with a bit of Shakespeare or a quote

28

from some famous play and I have to stop and think, yeah, he's quite a guy."

Three years ago the Taylors moved to Florida, where Dick had bought a radio station and opened an advertising agency. Holly, now seventeen, will finish high school in Key West. She plans to study communications in college and knows that her father will be delighted if she stays in broadcasting. "He never pushed me. I had done some things in school and a couple of shows at the Tennessee Williams Theater in Key West. When I finally said I wanted to stay in performing, he insisted that I get voice training and acting training. Once I made the decision he was right there to help."

Clearly the family connection to Flat Rock made it the obvious place to begin. But there are the emotional ties as well. "In some ways Flat Rock is more like home than Florida," says Holly. A certain dreamy quality comes into her voice. "Flat Rock is just always *there*. Even when I'm somewhere else. It's like a part of me."

While this spiritual connection to the place can be verified by dozens of actors who think of Flat Rock as a very special environment, there is nothing dreamy about the pace of work there. The new play starts on Wednesday morning. There is time for the cast to read through the script and talk about it briefly. But after lunch the new script must be put aside. Audiences have started to arrive for a matinee of the current show. Then there is the evening performance and it is Thursday morning before work on the new piece resumes. Thursday and Friday during the day the play is "blocked." The movements of the actors and the technical cues are set. If all has gone well, there will be time for a quick run-through on Saturday. But Saturday is another two-performance day. It is also "strike" night. During the evening performance the moment a costume or prop comes offstage for the last time it is immediately whisked away to storage to make room for the incoming

Holly played the maid in Heaven Can Wait *at Flat Rock. Her grandfather would have been proud to see her going into the family business.*

show. Before all the audience is out of the parking lot, most of the set has come down and apprentices are busy taking set-up orders from the technical director. The tech staff usually works round the clock. Sunday evening the entire company assembles for the first technical rehearsal. Light and sound cues are tried out and actors discover that furniture that was represented by folding chairs in rehearsal is now twice as large and three times as heavy as anticipated. Monday, during the day, solutions for all the problems that materialized Sunday night must be found because a full dress rehearsal is scheduled for that evening. Tuesday, during the day, there are cleanup rehearsals and a run-through, and on Tuesday evening the new play opens. On Wednesday morning another script is read, and what was the "new" play becomes the "current" play. And the process continues. There is an old piece of advice about acting in stock: "Learn your words and don't fall over the furniture."

Holly's first memory of the stage happened when she was five or six. She and her folks were on a summer visit and she wandered into the theater in the afternoon. It was Tuesday and a final rehearsal was in progress. On the stage an actor and actress were shouting at each other. Later, in the dining hall, she saw them sitting over their dinner laughing and friendly. That evening Holly was taken to her first performance, and here were the same actor and actress having the same argument they had had before. It looked like a wonderful way to make a living.

But beyond the profession itself, Holly feels a connection to her family history. "I've learned so much this summer," she says. "I've done three roles—the biggest one was a maid—and I've really fallen in love with acting. It's not just something I would like to do. I love it! If I wasn't sure when I came up here, I am now." And why not? It runs in the family.

AUTHOR'S NOTE: For a list of currently operating stock theaters, write to Actor's Equity Association. See Appendix D for the address.

3

Kimberly Eney

PAYING DUES

The salesclerk was frustrated. The tiny customer had narrowed the choice down to one of two scarves. Now she was taking too much time making up her mind. It would not have been too much time had the customer been an adult. But this was an eight-year-old girl. "Come on!" said the salesclerk with obvious impatience. "Make up your mind." Slowly and calmly the little girl eased the two scarves back across the counter toward the salesclerk. With a cool but pleasant smile she said, "Thank you, but I don't think I'll take either one today." And she turned and walked away.

Nearby in the Chicago department store, the little girl's father watched the scene with amusement and admiration. "She really wanted to buy a gift for her mother, but she was not going to be pressured into doing something just because someone else was pushing her."

Woody Eney tells the story today to illustrate one of the qualities he likes most about his daughter, Kimberly. Woody and Grey, Kimberly's mother, know that today, at sixteen, Kimberly is not going to be pressured into doing something she doesn't want to do. That is both the blessing and the curse of parenting this very attractive, witty, and intelligent young lady.

Kimberly Eney could easily exploit her beauty in Hollywood, but her father has other ideas.

It is a blessing in that they can count on Kim to use her own head in making choices. She is not likely to succumb to peer pressure. And because she knows they trust her judgment, she is open with her parents about the temptations around her. Recently while she was a student at a summer acting program she called her dad long distance. "Some of the kids are planning to sneak some beer into the dorm," she explained. "Would you be very upset if I tried some?" Woody knew that he could not prevent the temptation from being there. He also knew his daughter well enough to be able to count on her independence and objectivity.

In the world in which the Eneys live, that objectivity is important. Woody is a working actor in Hollywood. If his name does not ring a bell, his face will bring a spark of recognition for the dozens of commercials and television and film roles he has done. 'I'm a three-piece suit,"

At age ten Kim played a fairy in A Midsummer Night's Dream *at the Globe Theatre in Hollywood.*

says Woody, disparaging the long series of doctors, lawyers, and product spokesmen he has portrayed in front of the camera. Yet those who have seen him onstage know another side of his talent, for he is also a sensitive and commanding actor with great range and depth of technique.

It is no wonder. Woody took bachelor's and master's degrees at Virginia Commonwealth University. He then spent almost three years in London, England, at the Royal Academy of Dramatic Art. Returning to America, he proceeded to study for his Ph.D. in theater at Wayne State University in Detroit, Michigan. Yet he is not encouraging that kind of education for Kimberly unless she wants it or until she makes up her mind about just what kind of acting she wants to do. "For a woman it is still different. In Hollywood a woman can work from the time she is eighteen until she is about twenty-five. Then they start looking for someone with a younger jiggle to her behind. Unless she really knows how to act, her career is downhill after that."

And that is where the curse part of Kimberly's intelligent independence comes in. Hollywood can be very seductive, and Kimberly is honestly drawn to the glamour and riches of quick but temporary fame. Woody's relative success has allowed the family to taste some of the luxuries the film capital has to offer. Kim's school is a prime example. Woody and Grey became interested in the private high school when they read about the quality of education offered there. "Imagine," says Woody, "in this day and age a high school with three years of Latin! And a course in ancient Greek!" It was not until after Kimberly had enrolled that they began to realize just how "Hollywood" the school was. Gary Coleman of television's *Diff'rent Strokes* is a student there along with the children and/or grandchildren of some of Hollywood's biggest names. Woody was at the school one day when a large black Mercedes skidded out of the parking lot. "I said to Kim, 'He'd better be careful. He'll scratch his father's car.' She looked up and said, 'That's *his* car, Daddy.' What does a high school kid need with a fifty-thousand-dollar car?" Grudgingly Kimberly admits to the beginnings of an understanding of what her father is trying to say. "We have these great long 'discussions.' We don't have fights," she says with a mocking smile. "We have 'discussions.' " But her faith in her father's honesty and the open communication they share has helped her develop a more realistic approach to show business than most young people could have.

"In film it's so easy to say, 'Stop. Could we do that again,' " says Woody. "Onstage you've got to have the energy to keep going. I have a friend who plays softball twice a week just to keep himself competitive. If you don't have that edge, your performances can die, and then there goes your career. That's why I want Kimberly to get stage training. So she'll be able to really act when she can't jiggle anymore." He smiles and Kimberly laughs as she does so often at her father. But they both know there is a serious meaning in the joke.

Kimberly's first memory of the stage is from Houston, where Woody worked with the Alley Theater. She was only four at the time, and there was a graceful flower-bedecked swing on stage as part of the set for a Molière comedy. Between performances she would sit in it and swing out toward the empty seats. It was at that point she decided the stage could be a very comfortable place to be.

She started with dancing. But people kept saying, "So you're going to be a dancer like your mother!" One day Kim said to herself, "No, I'm not." Her reaction was as much from stubbornness as from the realization that she was not fully dedicated to that art form.

She was nine when the family moved to California. Between the higher-paying camera assignments, Woody found time to work with the Globe Theatre in Hollywood and Kimberly tagged along—only to find herself cast in a couple of Shakespearean shows. The thrill and energy of that happy swing in Houston returned to her, and before long it was clear that Kimberly Eney was going to be an actress. The major question was, would she jump onto the California bandwagon and exploit her youth and beauty or would she

Kim played a page boy in this production of Henry IV. *Woody, her father, is at the extreme left.*

take it seriously enough to learn the techniques and disciplines of her chosen craft. Would she "pay her dues"?

"It's hard for someone like me to work in movies right now," she says, ". . . ever since the *Twilight Zone* accident." She is referring to the death of two small children and star Vic Morrow during the filming of that movie when a helicopter fell on the scene. A blade decapitated Morrow and both children died from their injuries. There was a lot of talk about the producers skirting the juvenile work laws, and officials clamped down hard on safety conditions for anyone under eighteen. "They can get someone eighteen who looks younger to do anything I can do now," says Kim. "That way they don't have to worry about having a social worker on the set, or a teacher, or shorter work hours."

37

Still, Kimberly was not discouraged. There are plenty of sets that employ younger children and have to meet the juvenile regulations anyway. Kim could play her own age for them. So she set out to get an agent.

She made the rounds of agents' offices, leaving her picture at each one. Time and again the agents would take one look and say, "When you get the braces off your teeth, come back and see us." The braces were a problem. The agents couldn't see past them. But Kimberly has learned a lot from being around theater folk all her life. She went back to her photographer and had him airbrush the braces out of the pictures. Suddenly she got a lot more attention in the agents' offices and eventually signed with a representative. She was fifteen at the time and had done this all on her own.

The agent started sending her on commercial calls and a few producers called her back. On one call for a telephone company ad, they liked her very much but couldn't match her up with parents. Ironically they couldn't use her real father, since Woody already had a commercial running for a different company and one actor cannot represent two competing products.

At about this time Woody and Grey started having serious talks with Kim about her future. They never pressured her toward acting. In fact, they had avoided even encouraging her in that direction. But if she was going to undertake a career, certain rules had to be followed and Woody started pulling parental rank. She would have to learn to speak—not just project, but use her voice as an instrument with highs and lows and with texture and feeling. She would have to study character and role preparation. She would have to know how to use her body to speak when words were not telling the story. "She's good at that already," he says. "This morning we were having breakfast in a restaurant and the waiter started to reach for the menu. Kim was

Kim had her braces air-brushed out when the agents didn't like them.

very casual and she didn't even look at him. But she turned another page of the menu and kept reading. You could just see her saying, 'I'll give you the menu when I'm good and ready.' She didn't have to say anything."

The first stop on the training path was the summer session at the North Carolina School of the Arts in Winston-Salem. "I wanted to get her away from the Hollywood influence," Woody says. The program turned out to be a good sampling of the kind of thing her father had been talking about. There were gymnastics and stage combat. There were voice production and dance. And there were daily acting classes in which a variety of styles and approaches were explored. Kimberly had been on sets where actors waited all day to do a thirty-second piece of business. But this training was clearly designed to keep an actor going through an entire performance in front of hundreds of people instead of just a camera.

After the five-week session in North Carolina, Woody took Kimberly to New York for a saturation week of plays and musicals. Here she saw the very techniques

Kimberly says that she and her father don't have fights. They have "discussions."

she had just been studying put to use. She also saw some family friends playing roles that were nothing like the characters they played in California.

It was after the matinee of *Brighton Beach Memoirs* that Kimberly looked up at her father and said, "It's like waking up from a dream—coming outside after a play like that." They walked a few steps and Woody heard her quote Puck from *A Midsummer Night's Dream:* "If we shadows have offended, think but this—and all is mended—that you have but slumber'd here . . ." It was nice to have a teenage daughter who could quote Shakespeare. A little farther down the sidewalk Kimberly said, "You know, I could play the younger sister. With the right kind of training I could do that very well." And Woody smiled. Maybe, just maybe, he was finally getting through.

AUTHOR'S NOTE: For a list of professionally oriented training programs, see Appendix D.

4

Different Directions

TRACIE MON-TING LEE— Fair Lawn, New Jersey

It all happened so fast. One day Tracie was just another five-year-old playing with her baby sister in Fair Lawn, New Jersey. Then, only a few days later, here she was in Toronto, Canada, and the king was walking toward her, extending his hand and saying, "Hello, Tracie. I'm Yul Brynner." Tracie Mon-Ting Lee was about to begin a year as one of the king's children in Mr. Brynner's farewell tour of *The King and I*. The tour had been going on for several years, and now Tracie would travel with the show and be part of the final Broadway engagement.

It almost didn't happen. Judy Lee, Tracie's mother, got a letter from what was supposed to be a theatrical agency, which said that Tracie had come to their attention as a particularly charming child with a possible future in modeling. Judy was wisely cautious. It turned out that the company was in the business of selling overpriced photographs. There are several of these companies that use birth registrations and school re-

Tracie Lee on stage with the late Yul Brynner in The King and I. *(Tracie is seen at the right under Mr. Brynner's left hand.) (Photo, copyright by Henry Grossman)*

cords to make lists of children whose parents might pay too much for photographs they don't need on the chance that their child might have a career in the movies.

Judy backed off quickly, but the experience started her thinking. When Coral Leigh, a professional manager with solid legitimate credentials, announced open interviews in a local paper, Judy decided to take Tracie in.

Coral was delighted. It is somewhat unusual to find an Oriental family willing to have their child operate in the hectic and unsettled world of show business. Many families find the busy, independent life of a performer at odds with a heritage based on family order. Others, more recently immigrated, have so much trouble with the language that both contracts and scripts are beyond them. For this reason there seem to be fewer Oriental performers in the business and the competition is less intense and frustrating. The Lee family was very down to earth about the idea of Tracie working professionally. Peter Lee, with a background in engineering and a quiet but articulate manner, spoke warmly about giving Tracie every chance for new experiences. Judy had none of the pushy qualities often associated with stage mothers. Rather, with car keys and a baby in one hand and Tracie's hand in the other, she was a typical busy suburban housewife who just happened to be Chinese.

Coral first put Tracie through "the stretch." This is a game used with nonreaders to see if they can remember lines and maintain concentration. Tracie was asked to talk about something she liked. She spoke about her teddy bear. Then Coral asked her to repeat something she had said about the toy. She did. Coral added a phrase to the phrase that Tracie had started and Tracie repeated that word for word. Another phrase was added and Tracie continued to keep all her "lines" in place. Back and forth the game went until Coral was amazed by the ability of this tiny child to pick up quickly almost any direction she was given.

Tracie Lee

Tracie uses this picture to send to producers and directors. Her manager, Coral Leigh, has these pictures printed one hundred at a time.

Tracie got the first job she was sent up for. It was a Jell-O Pudding Pop commercial with Bill Cosby, and it went so well that a few days after the filming Coral called Judy to set up an interview for *The King and I*. Judy laughed. Just before Tracie had been born, Peter and Judy had gone to see Yul Brynner in the very first part of this *King and I* tour. Judy had been struck by the possibility that the baby she was carrying might someday perform in a production of *The King and I*, never knowing that thought would become a reality five years later in the very same production.

When Tracie was offered the job, Peter and Judy had to do a lot of thinking very quickly. Judy and the baby would have to travel with Tracie for over half a year. Tracie was about to start school in the fall. What would it mean for her formal education to take place in a dressing room at a theater instead of in a classroom? She had already started gymnastics classes. She would be a year behind the others in her group before this project was over. She had also begun piano lessons. There would be no time for them on the road. And what about the people involved? Would Tracie be exposed to language and activities, values and attitudes that were at odds with the behavior she was used to at home? Was she ready for that? The only way to find out was to do it.

The plan was simple. Seven children were hired for the tour. In each tour city an advance director had hired seven local children so that the king would always have fourteen children at every performance. The full-time children were to partner the local children and guide them through the four scenes in which the family appeared. Tracie was replacing one of this touring group. In Toronto she would be treated like one of the new kids with an experienced partner of her own. After that she would be expected to show a new performer in each city how to get through the complex show.

There was a lot to learn. The children make their first entrance to the musical "March of the Siamese Children." They bow before the king and then take their place onstage kneeling. When all the children are in place, there is the sound of a great gong and everyone bows their head to the floor. Tracie was warned that if anyone's head was not all the way down, Mr. Brynner would snap his fingers. This little action would not be seen by the audience, but as soon as the scene was over, the offending child could count on a good talking-to by one of the stage managers.

After this introduction there is a schoolroom scene in which everyone sings "Getting to Know You." The children are again onstage for the end of the first act,

Tracie (top) *with Peter, Judy, and the baby.*

and they are gathered around the bed of the dying king at the end of the play. In that scene one of the princesses makes a touching appeal to "Mrs. Anna," the English schoolteacher, not to leave Siam. Tracie was asked to understudy this important little role and got to play it several times both on the road and during the Broadway run.

The tour went on for over six months. The show had arranged for a teacher, Miss Malone, to travel with the company, and each day except Monday there was school. There were also visits to places of interest in every city. In Chicago there was a newspaper plant. In Cleveland there was a wonderful museum. In Boston they visited historic sites.

Finally the long tour was over and the company settled in to a six-month run on Broadway that would be Mr. Brynner's last performances as the character that had made him famous. Tracie was delighted to be back home in her own room every night. She hadn't realized how much she missed her old friends and playing in her own backyard.

The schedule was still hectic. She was up for school every morning and had to come directly home for a nap and light meal before her mother or father drove her into New York for the nightly performance. After the

All of the King and I *kids dressed in a large room on the top floor of the Broadway Theatre. Here Tracie checks out one of the three costumes she wore in the show.*

show there was the drive home and she was seldom in bed before midnight. On Wednesday and Saturday afternoons there were matinees, and between shows the children in the cast would often have a short play time in Central Park. But then it was right back to the theater. Eight times a week nearly two thousand people would gather expecting Yul Brynner—and Tracie Lee—to do *The King and I*.

On June 30, 1985, *The King and I* closed, and life in the Lee home began to return to normal. Tracie's family is proud of her for the maturity and discipline she has learned. They know that this sense of dedication will be a valuable asset all her life. Tracie, on the other hand, takes it more lightly. It was fun, it was hard, and it was tiring. She is glad to have a rest. "But," she says, "after a while I'll probably get bored with things and want to be in another play." With her looks and charm, her energy, and now her experience, it is likely she will be in many more, if she wants to be.

MATTHEW BRODERICK— New York, New York

There is a sparkle of innocent mirth in the familiar eyes. We've seen them in *WarGames* and *Ladyhawke* and *Max Dugan Returns*. The eyes are mirthful, yet there is a carefully trained observer behind them. The eyes are the first thing we recognize when Matthew Broderick turns to the audience and gets his first laugh in Neil Simon's *Biloxi Blues*. Eugene, the character he plays, is a stand-in for Neil Simon himself in this second autobiographical play. Broderick played him first in *Brighton Beach Memoirs* and won a Tony award for the effort. When *Biloxi Blues,* the comedy hit of the 1985 Broadway season, came along, there was no contest for the starring role.

While the play is very funny, there is a serious bit of self-analysis tucked between the laughs. Eugene is an observer rather than a participant. Eugene is cautious rather than assertive. Eugene is careful where others might take risks. All this was true of the young Neil Simon. Much of it can also be said of Matthew Broderick. Perhaps that is why he is so good in the role.

On his first day of school Matthew was handed a form to fill out for a library card. In the blank space marked "occupation" he wrote "actor." It is easy to see why. His father, James Broderick, was a working actor. A working actor is different from a star. A star plays leads and is usually very careful about which roles to take. A star may wait months or even years between projects because the material is not exactly what is expected by the star's public. Yet people come to see stars no matter what they are in. That's what makes them stars. A working actor, on the other hand, usually plays supporting roles and doesn't have to be too worried about public image. A working actor usually has more work than a star simply because there are more supporting roles than star roles. Occasionally a working actor will get a chance to be a star, as James Broderick did playing the father in the popular television series *Family*. But people who recognized him in *Family* could remember him playing dozens of neighbors to the star, or police chief to the star detective, or doctor to the sick star. Onstage he was a popular figure with both audiences and other actors. His easygoing manner and generous smile made him a good friend to have on a tour, and he toured often. During summers he would take little Matthew with him while Patricia, wife, mother, and artist, stayed in her studio back in New York. Matthew can remember being something of a "puppy" to the people backstage. Actors and crew members were usually indulgent with this wide-eyed boy who played quietly in his father's dressing room during performances. The boy, in the meantime, was soaking up the atmosphere of the theater and carefully filing away little pieces of information and observations about how different actors worked, how various moments could be played, and what constituted professional behavior on and off the stage. But with the exception of a couple of outings with his father, Matthew stayed away from the stage itself. He wanted to be an actor. He had more experience in theaters than many working professionals. Yet the thought of standing in front of an audience was terrifying to him.

At Walden, a New York high school noted for its theater program, he spent his first year just watching, afraid even to audition. In his second year he finally mustered enough courage to read for the part of Wall in *A Midsummer Night's Dream*. He got the part and realized that now he would have to play it. Sheer terror followed him throughout rehearsals until the harsh brightness of rehearsal lighting was replaced by the rich warmth of stage lights during the final run-throughs.

Matthew Broderick (right) *with Tommy Tune* (left) *and Harvey Fierstein* (center). *In accepting the Tony award Matthew honored his father. Most of the audience at the Schubert Theatre had known James Broderick and it was an emotional moment for everyone concerned. (UPI/Bettmann Newsphotos)*

Suddenly this arrangement of actor-bathed-in-light facing audience-gathered-in-darkness felt very good. Perhaps the light was a barrier to keep the fear away. Or perhaps a kind of environmental destiny based on a lifetime of being around actors finally took hold. Whatever happened on that stage at Walden, Matthew remembers that he got better and better at theater and worse and worse at school. By graduation time he was determined to give acting a chance before trying college. He never made it to college.

There were a few off-Broadway roles and a movie that never got finished before he read for Neil Simon for *Brighton Beach.* It took a while. First he read from the stage script. Then he was handed a film script. He read from one, then from the other. After he left the audition he called his agent. "You had a good day," she said.

"I got the play?" asked Matthew.

"You got them both," said the agent.

That summer, while they were filming *Max Dugan Returns*, James Broderick got sick. Before the Tony award was given to Matthew for best actor in *Brighton Beach Memoirs*, his father died. He never got to see his son in *WarGames* or in *1918* or in *Ladyhawke*, and he never got to see the sign high above Broadway that reads MATTHEW BRODERICK IN NEIL SIMON'S BILOXI BLUES. When they put your name above the title it means that you're a star. James Broderick, working actor, never got to see his son become a star.

Today Matthew Broderick is casual about his success. "Every time I've gotten a job it's been through luck," he says. "You can't make that happen." True. But when the luck came, Matthew was ready for it with a combination of natural talent and a lifetime of observation. He was lucky to grow up in the theater, but he has worked hard to feed that experience into his career. Some of his opportunities have come by chance. But he has been ready to act on those chance happenings and turn them into solid career moves. And audiences who have been charmed by his warmth and humor and vulnerability hope he keeps on getting lucky.

JOE KRUFT—
Cosmopolis, Washington

"I don't like this!" The speaker was an adult.

"Well, I admit it's unusual. But you have to admit he's done everything we required." Another adult was speaking.

"But he's only fourteen years old!" said the first. "Our by-laws say he has to be eighteen."

"So we turn him down on the basis of his age?"

"Yes," said the adult, "we turn him down."

Fourteen-year-old Joe Kruft was disappointed when the people in charge of the Driftwood Players turned down his application to direct a major production for the company. Driftwood is a community theater in Aberdeen, Washington, governed by a board of directors and a strict set of by-laws which dictate how a person qualifies to direct major productions. First the applicant has to work as an assistant director on a main stage show. Joe had done that. Then he or she has to stage-manage a production, taking full responsibility for supervising both the actors onstage and the backstage staff. Joe had done that when he was thirteen. Next the applicant must direct a workshop production of a one-act play and present it to the board. Joe had done that, and everyone who saw his show was impressed. In particular the actors found his direction as insightful and constructive as any they had had from adult directors.

And why not? At fourteen Joe has already had as much experience in theater as most of the adults he has worked with. At eight he played his first community theater role—young Scrooge in *A Christmas Carol*. He had sung most of his life, but playing a character in a play gave him an opportunity to put together for the

At the age of ten Joe Kruft played young Patrick in Auntie Mame *for the Driftwood Players. Now he directs for the same company.*

first time his natural talent and his intense desire to communicate. Young Scrooge was followed almost immediately with young Patrick in *Auntie Mame* and the list just got longer and longer.

There are three theaters in the area around Cosmopolis, Washington, where Joe lives with his father, an electrical lineman, his mother, and a younger sister. Joe haunted them all, playing roles, working backstage, soaking up the atmosphere and the potential of the stage. His family became involved. His father started

Joe has tried to develop all his talents. Here he sings in a musical revue.

running lights for productions Joe was in. His mother arranged costumes and helped backstage. His sister began acting too. It was the only way they ever got to see Joe. Almost all his time was centered on this second set of homes. Yes, he went to school. Yes, he played golf occasionally. But most of his energy was focused on acting.

When he was twelve Joe read about the Karen Kramer Drama Program in Seattle, one hundred fifty miles away. It was a summer program for young people set up by Karen Kramer and Stanley Kramer, the film director, and conducted by theater professionals. Accepted into the program, Joe blossomed. Linda Hartzel, director of the Seattle Children's Theatre, worked with Joe that summer and has continued to be both mentor and friend. "He's amazing," she says. "He's read everything ever written about the theater. He's a very talented performer. And I think what he's done is fantastic."

"What he's done" is to come back from Seattle with a firm desire to learn directing in addition to acting. In pursuit of that dream he set about qualifying to become a director for the Driftwood Players.

He was rejected on the basis of his age only. But Joe Kruft is not one to dwell on defeat. With the same

Hollywood star Dom DeLuise was a guest speaker at the Karen Kramer Drama Program. As always, Joe (right) *tried to soak up all he could.*

mixture of assurance and optimism that marks all his work, he arranged a loan of fifteen hundred dollars and set about creating his own company. He selected *Send Me No Flowers* for his project and secured the rights. His father and mother said they would help, and the phone started ringing with offers of assistance from dozens of people who had admired his work with the other theaters in the area. He put together a cast ranging in age from eighteen to sixty. Many of those people were among the most experienced actors in the area. They, like Linda Hartzel in Seattle, had found that no matter his age, they could learn from Joe Kruft and they enjoyed his fresh, confident manner. Joe was well on his way to becomng a successful producer/director.

It was ironic that the board of the Driftwood Players then decided to review Joe's application to direct. After all, there were already three theaters in the area competing for the same talent and the same audience. The outcome of that review was that *Send Me No Flowers* directed by Joe Kruft opened the Driftwood Players' 1985–86 season.

Joe looks forward to the day when he can make a living acting and directing, but he hasn't made any firm plans about the future. He has to finish high school first. What he is sure about is the fact that the support of his family and friends has been an essential part of his success to date. Clearly he is surrounded by people who recognize his talent, his drive, and his potential for personal and professional success. Clear also is the fact that Joe Kruft is a young man who has made his life decisions early and has systematically set about using every available resource to turn his dreams into reality.

ZACHARY STIER—
Cincinnati, Ohio

The telephone rang abruptly and Jane Stier stopped playing the piano and walked across the room to answer it. The room was large as the house was large. Not a fancy house, but a large old comfortable house, the kind that helped make playing the piano and raising two children and having a yard and living in Cincinnati joyful and graceful and fulfilling for Jane.

"Hello," she said into the receiver.

"Jane, this is Nancy Carson in New York."

"Hi, Nancy. What's up?"

"Can you and Zach fly in tomorrow? I've got something that may be just right for him."

"Sure," said Jane, "what time?"

And the two women worked out the details of another audition trip for Zachary Stier, eleven-year-old professional actor, living quietly on Wood Avenue in Cincinnati but traveling wherever and whenever the jobs demand.

"It really is that simple," Jane said in a recent interview. "Nancy, Zach's agent, just calls up and we go. She's very good about not wasting our time and money. She calls only if it's something Zach is really right for."

This particular time it is for a musical version of *Our Town* called *Grover's Corners*. The production will rehearse for two months in New York, tour for a few months to get the bugs out, and then come to Broadway.

On the plane the next day Zachary sits quietly and looks out the window. His nature is quiet, and he doesn't make a big thing out of his professional work. "I guess a lot of our neighbors don't even know what I do. I just disappear every now and then."

While Zachary Stier lives quietly in Cincinnati, Nancy Carson, his agent in New York, uses this picture to get him work.

Zach's school doesn't mind these trips. In the first place it is an arts magnet school for the Cincinnati district. The School for Creative and Performing Arts was set up by the public school system to encourage artistically talented students like Zachary. In the second place Zach's dad, Harold, heads the math department at the school, where both Zach and his older sister, Amy, are enrolled. In the third place Zach has nearly perfect grades, in spite of frequent days off for auditions and commercial shoots and occasional extended leaves for productions out of town.

"Did your dad print up a new résumé for you?" asks Jane as the now familiar hum of the jets urges them eastward. Zach reaches into their carryall and shows his mother the freshly revised and processed sheet. During one extended absence Zach and Amy and Jane surprised Harold with a home computer with a word processing function to help keep that part of the family busy while the other part was on tour.

The résumé is neatly arranged and spaced and lists Zach's personal description, address and phone number, and credits. There are commercials and professional training listed. There is the Young People's Special *Rosie,* in which Zach played Jeff for television. There are the various Cincinnati credits such as Amahl in *Amahl and the Night Visitors* with the Cincinnati Opera, and at the top of the list there is *"Oliver! . . .* Broadway."

Actually the 1984 revival of *Oliver!* was not Zach's first production of the musical version of Charles Dickens's *Oliver Twist.* The year before, the artistic director of Zach and Amy's school had been asked to choreograph a professional touring production of the show. He used a number of his students from the arts magnet school and after an audition in Cincinnati the director asked Zach to play the title role.

Jane and Harold were pleased and supportive. Although Harold is a mathematician and educator by trade, he is also an appreciative and enthusiastic supporter of the arts. Jane took a degree in piano performance and has been a musician all her life. They are both glad to see their children continue their love and involvement with arts.

Since Zach was only nine at the time, Jane decided to go on tour with him and was hired to be an official chaperon for the young cast. Soon after the three-month tour, word reached the Stiers that a Broadway revival was being prepared. Harold, excited by the enthusiasm that Zach had shown for the work and proud of the flexibility the school had shown, called the casting director in New York and arranged an audition for his son.

Zach's clear, sensitive voice and charming personality were greeted with open arms in New York, and he was asked to understudy the title role and play one of the gang of child pickpockets who people the story.

Again Jane and Zach left Cincinnati—this time for New York. They took a six-month sublease on an apartment in the city in anticipation of a healthy run. Rehearsals went smoothly since Zach already knew the

In his first production of Oliver! Zach toured around the
country. In costume he looks the part of the street kid
Dickens created.

material well from his previous engagement. The show opened, but the reviews were less than had been hoped for. The advertising campaign did not work, and two weeks later *Oliver!* closed. Less than two months after it began, the adventure was over.

Jane's first instinct was to pack up and head home. But Zach pointed out that they would have to pay for the apartment whether they stayed in New York or not, so they might as well take advantage of the situation and hang around for a while at least.

New York can be an education in itself. Mother and son went to museums and galleries, television studios and Broadway shows. Usually working actors get frustrated by the fact that they never get to see other shows because they all perform at the same time. After *Oliver!* closed they had a chance to see everything they wanted to see.

They also used the time for professional advancement. "It was obvious right from the first that Zach liked this work. Since we had the time, there was no reason not to see just how far he could go." They made appointments with several agents and interviewed them. The personal and professional rapport with Nancy Carson was the best, and they came to a management agreement with her. Since then she has called them into the city every few weeks as job possibilities have come up.

On the plane home from the *Grover's Corners* audition, Jane turns to her handsome son. "How do you think it went?"

Zach smiles and says with a calm acceptance of the situation, "I think they really want someone older."

"I think you're right," says Jane. As it turned out, he was accurate in his assessment and that was the end of that.

Most recently Nancy brought the Stiers to New York to audition for a touring production of the musical version of *The Yearling*. Zach was cast as Fodderwing,

Zachary in rehearsal. There is a combination of outgoing charm and inward calm in him that is most appealing, as this picture shows.

the crippled boy who names the deer and dies in the second act. The play was scheduled to rehearse in New York, open in Atlanta, and tour to Texas after that.

In the midtown hotel room that was home during the New York rehearsals for *The Yearling*, the Stiers welcomed the interviewer with poise and grace. At eleven Zachary is an attractive and charming boy. He is quiet and given more to chess and reading than to rough sports or rock music. He takes his talent gently and avoids the kind of temperament child actors are often plagued with. His mother seems a gentle person too.

"Zach and Amy have grown up in a very loving home," she says. "And they know that if they decide they don't want to do this anymore, it's all right with us. They are doing this because they want to."

In *The Yearling* Fodderwing's death is portrayed with projections. Earlier in the show the little boy sings of his dream of flying high in the sky. When he dies, the music of that song accompanies a series of slides in which Fodderwing's picture is surrounded by feathers. The image changes from that of a boy into that of a bird. It is a graceful, poised, gentle moment. And it is not hard to see why the producers of *The Yearling* recognized in Zachary Stier the qualities that would bring that image to life.

5

Marianne Hyatt

ACTING OPENS A DOOR

The visitor stands in sheer awe. There before the eye the land drops away and then rises in a series of ruffled formations that gather themselves up to the tops of mesas and buttes. "Spanish skirts" they are sometimes called. Layer on layer of color wrap around the landscape in expanding bands that look like the fluttering laces of a flamenco dancer. But these ruffles do not flutter. They are solid stone and weathered by a million years of wind from the desert plain and water from the tributaries of the Red River.

As the visitor makes his way down the steps to a seat in the open air arena, the land rises all around. The canyon itself forms a backdrop for the stage, and the evening sun disappearing behind the rim of this scenic masterpiece paints the rock with a thousand shades of orange, then red, and then the deep purple of night.

The play begins. Like the state it portrays, it is called *Texas*. It was written by Paul Green and tells the story of the romance, heroism, and determination of the people of this panhandle region. Green was known as the "father of outdoor drama." First in coastal North Carolina with *The Lost Colony* about the first English attempts to settle the New World, and later with nearly twenty other scripts, he, more than any writer, has tied the history of people to the places where that history took place. Each of his dramas was written to be performed on the very spot where the characters lived and made their contributions to the past and the present.

Surely there is not a more dramatic setting than this wild expanse of canyon known as Palo Dura. And surely there is drama in the story of a schoolteacher from the "civilized" streets and sidewalks of St. Louis who arrives in this frontier wilderness and learns to embrace the wildness and respect the open, uninhibited people who have settled it. The character is Elsie McLean. She makes her entrance on an actual train which chugs onstage with the steam and smoke of the nineteenth century. Elsie thinks she is bringing change to the Wild West. It is the West that changes her. The actress is Marianne Hyatt, and her story is not unlike Elsie's.

Marianne always sang and danced. She acted some too. But more than that she sang, and most of all she danced. Growing up in Texas, first in Richardson, near Dallas, and later in Amarillo, where the family moved when she was sixteen, Marianne danced. Her father, who works for an oil company, and her mother, who runs a bridge studio and plays master point bridge, headed a household of energetic girls. The youngest was forever playing volleyball and other team sports. The middle girl developed as a gymnast. Marianne, the eldest, always danced. "No one was ever at home," laughs Marianne today.

In Dallas she studied with the Metropolitan Ballet, taking as many classes each week as her busy parents could get her to. From the age of eight she spent as much time in tights and leotards as in all her other clothes combined. In Amarillo, with eight years of training behind her, she joined the Lone Star Ballet and continued to study and perform. Summers she spent in San Francisco or New York studying dance.

Marianne Hyatt (center) *during a performance of* Texas. *The Palo Dura Canyon serves as the backdrop for the show.*

The discipline she was learning as a performer and as a person made her a good candidate for adult roles in her high school. She played the lead in *Up the Down Staircase*, the role of a teacher, and won an award for the effort. Yet there was something in her that was restless and untamed. There was a freedom in her that was at odds with the serious control the years of study had imposed.

After high school Marianne headed for Boston. With ten years of study behind her, she auditioned for the Boston Ballet. As part of the Second Company, she had a chance to both study and perform. But the Second Company closed and the main company was not taking on new performers. She was offered a job in Chicago

Marianne dances with Perry Brown in the Lone Star Ballet production of The Nutcracker.

with the Ruth Page *Nutcracker,* a seasonal production of the Chicago Ballet Company. When the holiday season was over, it was back to Boston, and since the job market there had dried up, she went on to New York. There were a lot of classes that cost a lot of money. But there were no dance jobs to pay for them.

Doubt began to set in. It is the performer's constant companion, and in times of stress and the absence of work, doubt can dominate a performer's life.

In Marianne's case the doubt settled over the whole idea of dance. She had been a dancer for so long. She had put so much time and energy and money into a career in dance that at some point she had stopped even asking if it made her happy. "I was like a horse with blinders on," she says. "Somehow I was supposed to be a dancer whether I liked it or not."

New York turns gray from December until April. Gray-faced people walk gray sidewalks beside cold gray streets. The rain is gray and so is the snow after the first clean hour or two. Even the sunshine of the few clear

67

days has a grayish cast to it. All through that long cold winter Marianne made the daily trudge to the studio in the West Sixties where she studied. But her mood and her outlook were as gray as the streets and the sky.

When the opportunity to audition for a musical revue for a summer stock tour came along, she decided to go. She prepared her music and made her way to the studio where the audition was to be held. She knew she would have to sing. She knew she would have to act. She hoped she could impress them with her dancing.

The stage manager ushered her into the tiny studio and watched the lovely delicate features of her face fall when she realized there was not enough room to show off her dancing. She gave her music to the piano player and turned to face the director. The music started, but Marianne didn't. Something like panic had erased her mind the way a magnet erases recording tape. No words. No melody. Nothing would come out. She thought it was all over. She thought for a moment that all she could do was dance and she knew that didn't make her fulfilled, or happy, or employed. But then the director was working with her, getting her to relax. The musical director started her music again, and before long the audition was finished. To her surprise, they liked her. A few days later the contract was signed. Then they went into rehearsals and opened the show for a limited run. Within little more than a month the whole show was over. Marianne went back home to Amarillo.

She had made a decision. She could no longer think of herself as just a classical dancer. If she was going to do more—if she was going to think of herself as a triple threat actress-singer-dancer—then she needed more training. She enrolled at the University of Texas in Austin. The drama program there is demanding and detailed. Every aspect of acting is explored, from improvisation to the fine points of Shakespearean performance. There is even a required course in the history of furniture design so that students can know how and why various periods demand various body postures.

Acting has opened a whole new world to Marianne. "Dance is raw physical energy," she says. "If your body is strong, it is easy to control that energy. But acting is more subtle. You have to motivate your mind to learn to focus your energy in a very different way in order to relate to other people."

The change to acting as a primary art form has also made it clear that discipline and work are still principal components of the performer's life-style. Marianne's daily schedule while playing the lead in *Texas* is typical of any actress playing a leading musical role whether on Broadway or in the Palo Dura Canyon. She sleeps until 10:00 A.M., not because she is lazy, but because she needs as much rest as possible. First thing in the morning she bicycles to the gym for a two-hour workout with weights, followed by aerobic training for breath support and vocal projection to the two thousand people who fill the unmiked outdoor theater each night. After a light lunch she takes two dance classes to keep her body toned and flexible. The stage at Palo Dura is nearly one hundred feet wide, and crossing it with both speed and grace requires great physical control. After some rest she is off to the theater, arriving at about 6:30. There is some social time with cast and crew members before the company vocal warmup at 7:00. This singing exercise accomplishes two goals. Obviously it shapes up the voices for the musical aspects of the show. Less obvious, but just as important, is the unity among cast members it helps promote. Even though the company of some eighty actors and fifty technicians and support personnel are all well-rehearsed and know their jobs, the warmup gives the cast a chance to put aside the other events of the day and focus their attention on this particular performance.

Marianne and two other actresses cross behind the great stage in Texas. Moving and speaking in such a large space takes unusual physical and vocal skill.

Marianne takes personal charge of placing her costumes in the various locations around the theater where she must change during the fast-moving show. After makeup a company meeting for notes at 8:00 leaves her just a few minutes before the 8:30 curtain time.

During this time she often thinks about her new beginning in acting. "I feel different about myself now. I'm happier. I've found there's such a range of strengths in me."

She thinks about her future. She would like to use her talents on the stage. She can see herself in a Broadway musical. But she can also see herself traveling and expanding as a person. She has found that the more fully she lives her life, the more she has to bring to the stage. The more completely she understands herself as a person, the more completely she is able to fill out the personality of the character she is playing.

She also thinks about her character. Elsie is a young woman who has grown up with a very limited set of expectations about what civilization is. In St. Louis the possibilities were as carefully laid out as the orderly streets and sidewalks. In Texas she learns to "hear the music in the wind," not just in her piano. She learns the beauty of open space and open friendship. And she learns that what seemed at first to be a hostile and foreign environment can in fact become a new home. These are qualities Marianne feels well prepared to play.

AUTHOR'S NOTE: For the cost of postage, the Institute of Outdoor Drama will mail an up-to-date list of outdoor dramas all over the country. See Appendix D for the address.

6

Jessica Long

AN ENTERTAINING
PARTNERSHIP

In the darkness the small orchestra plays the final climactic notes of the Act I score. The audience applauds enthusiastically for the performers who have just completed the first part of *Gypsy*, and stop only when the house lights come up and the waiters start moving around among the tables serving intermission drinks and coffee to the patrons. The sound of the applause is quickly replaced by the chatter of excited voices and the clinking of glasses and cups.

At a table on the top level, two middle-aged couples thank the waiter for their refreshments. "Isn't this fun!" says one of the women.

"I think it's great!" says the man opposite her. "I'm glad you suggested it."

"Oh, we come out here all the time," says the woman. "It really makes sense—having your meal and a show all in one place. You don't even have to get up from the table."

"Except to go to the buffet. I've never seen so much food in all my life!" This is from the other woman. "And I love the way they have the food tables set up right on the stage and then just take it all away when the show starts."

"What did you think of the show?" asks the other man.

"I think it's just great," says his friend.

Near them at the head of the aisle David Long listens. He likes to listen to the comments the theatergoers make at intermission. Much of the conversation is the same night after night, but he listens anyway, waiting to hear the discussions turn in the direction he is interested in.

"What did you think of that little girl?" asks one of the women.

"You mean the one that looks like Shirley Temple?" David's attention has zeroed in on this bit of conversation.

"I've never seen anything like her," came the reply. "She's so tiny. But she dances like . . . like Shirley Temple!"

"Better," says the man. "She's really terrific. Sings, dances, and she really got me with her acting. We saw her in *Annie* down in Naples last year. Same thing. She's a terrific little actress. Jessica something. Let me see that program. Jessica . . . yes, here it is. Jessica Long."

"What did you think, George?" asks one of the women.

"Great!" says the man. "I think she's just great."

If dinner theater audiences are not the most experienced theatergoers around, they are at the very least an enthusiastic and appreciative population. The dinner theater movement in America began in the late 1950s and blossomed during the following decade. The idea was simple: Combine a sizable meal (usually an "all you can eat" buffet) with a light comedy or musical play all in one place. As the idea caught on, the attendance figures grew. With them grew a sophistication in both the quality of production and the level of expertise among the performers. At first dinner theaters were

Jessica Long as Baby June in Gypsy. *In both her look and her style, Jess is often compared to Shirley Temple.*

frowned on by purists as a kind of nightclub act. But today dinner theater stages provide a respected work outlet for everyone from beginners to some of the most celebrated stars in the theatrical sky. One of the primary areas for dinner theater growth has been Florida, where a largely older population currently supports about two dozen professional dinner theater operations.

In this environment the career of Jessica Long has begun to flourish. Although Jessica is only twelve years old, she has already amassed a long list of theatrical credits and has taken advantage of a support system that allows her to grow nightly on stages all over the state in front of warm and responsive audiences.

It is Jessica's father, David, who helps make her professional growth possible. It is David Long who sits

74

at the back night after night and watches the performance and listens to the intermission talk. "I can't just drop her off and come back later to pick her up. Some theaters we have worked in are an hour and a half's drive away. If I tried to go home, I'd just have to turn around and come back. You can only do so much shopping during an evening. So mostly I just wait around and watch the show."

David does more than that. He acts as manager for both Jessica and younger brother, Thatcher, who also acts. He reads trade papers and notices of auditions. He gets his children to and from dance classes and singing classes and auditions and rehearsals and performances. He maintains files of every newspaper mention of their names. He has developed a network of some sixty theater, film, and television producers in the region and periodically sends new pictures or copies of press clippings or updated résumés to them. Yet, according to Chris Parsons, artistic director of the Naples Dinner Theater, David is not a pushy stage parent. "He never says a word during rehearsals," says Parsons. "He never interferes in any way with the production. But every time I turn around in the office, there's a little note from David about something Jess is doing. Or a new picture or a copy of a good review. When I think about doing a show with kids in it, I can't help but think of Jessica."

Most professional actors would be delighted to have a manager so conscientious—or the discipline to keep the mailings up themselves. According to Parsons, he doesn't resent all the promotional material that comes from Cape Coral, where the Longs live. "It's just good business," Parsons emphasizes. "I like Jessica. I know that she's very, very talented. And I'm always glad to hear she's working."

Parsons was the first professional director to recognize in Jessica the special quality that separates the young professional from the talented amateur. "I cast her as one of the children in *The King and I* when she

A tired Jessica leaves the theater after a performance. Her father usually drives her to the theater, waits during the show, and drives her home.

was nine and I could tell right away. All you have to do with Jess is tell her what you want and she does it. Particularly with dance. My wife choreographs our shows and she uses Jess to show the other kids what to do. She'll give Jess a combination and let her stand in front. Then she can work with the other kids while they follow what Jess is doing."

Jessica has studied dance since she was four, first in Michigan and later in Florida, where the family moved seven years ago. She has gravitated to teachers who encourage their students to partake in various regional and national dance competitions. "I like the competitions," says tiny Jessica, who could pass for eight or nine even now that she is developing a more mature look. "Not just the prizes." (She has won a wall full.) "I like the travel, seeing new places, and meeting new people and entertaining them." She admits to thinking about being a pediatrician when she grows up, but thinks acting may well win out over medicine.

The competitions in dance, gymnastics, and roller skating have given Jessica an ability to focus on the work at hand. She doesn't waste time or energy on fear or personal feelings or outside distractions. She can enter a situation, size up the needs of the moment, and concentrate all her resources on accomplishing the goal at hand. The story of a commercial audition puts this into perspective. She was called to read for a spot promoting a local barbecue restaurant. The producer was seeing several children for the job. He had already had to coach several of them through the short bit of dialogue, and his patience was wearing thin. When Jessica walked in, she already knew what the product was and had seen previous commercials for the same outfit. The producer handed her the copy and asked if Jessica wanted some time to look it over. "No," she said without looking up from scanning the page. "Do you want this with an accent or without?" The producer was struck by both her immediate grasp of the concept of the piece and her clear desire to waste neither his time nor her own. She added a bit of "country" to her clear, unaccented speech and, needless to say, she got the job.

The competitions have given Jessica another valuable asset—exposure. During a national dance competition in New York, she attracted the attention of a New York talent agency that is currently grooming her for Broadway auditions.

The dinner theaters in Florida have a special fondness for plays and musicals with children in them. Perhaps the high percentage of retired grandparents in the state helps account for this. Or it may be the universal appeal of attractive, talented youngsters. Whatever the reason, shows like *Annie, The Sound of Music, Gypsy,* and *The King and I* appear on the schedules of many of the Florida stages with some regularity. Jessica had already done one *Gypsy* when the Mark One Dinner Theatre in Lakeland asked her to

The Long family: Thatcher (left), *Jane, David, and Jess.*

play Baby June in its production. This meant a six-week relocation for Jess and her dad. But she was still able to get in two days of school a week. Sunday after the performance they would drive home to Cape Coral. Tuesday after school they would drive back to Lakeland for the evening show.

Jessica was able to maintain her good grades during this time because she has learned to do whatever needs to be done in order to go on with her performing. And she has had the good fortune to have a parent who is able to help her every step of the way. But that help has been purchased at a high price. David Long's body is slowly being crushed by a nerve disorder that could eventually make his limbs useless.

When David was a child he did not have the option to dance and sing and act. He was a victim of polio, a disease that devastated America and crippled or killed thousands of children during the 1950s. David survived the disease with no serious ill effects and grew into healthy adulthood. He married, and he and his wife had

Jessica as Kim with Steve Daniels as Captain Andy in Showboat. *This is one of several shows she has done at the Naples Dinner Theater under the direction of Christopher Parsons.*

two children—Jessica and Thatcher. He worked for the United States Postal Service. His wife worked as a teacher's aide. They were a simple, happy family.

Then in the mid-1970s David began to notice pain and weakness in his hands. Doctors identified the problem as a form of nerve degeneration related to his childhood polio. They warned him that the more he used his hands the more useless they would become. He was able to retire from the postal service on a disability pension, and the family moved from Michigan to Florida, where the physical requirements of day-to-day living would be simpler.

With an income and plenty of time, David poured himself into his children. He would help them at anything they wanted to do. They wanted to study dance. He became their chauffeur. They wanted to perform. He became their manager. They needed to travel. He became their escort.

Today the condition has progressed into his legs and his neck. But David is philosophical. "I still have a few more years to give my children," he says. "By that time maybe they can do all of this on their own."

Back at the theater the waiters have cleared the intermission glasses and the musicians have moved back into position. The house lights have begun to dim and the two couples near the back, like the rest of the audience, have become quiet, waiting for the second act to begin.

In the shadows David Long listens to the music. *Gypsy* is the story of a stage mother who lives her life through the children she forces onto the stage. David is not like that. He doesn't want his children to have his life. He doesn't want to make their decisions for them. Like most parents, he wants them to make their own choices, and he wants the chance to help them accomplish their goals for as long as he is able.

The orchestra plays "Everything's Coming Up Roses." For Jessica and her brother and for David Long, right now everything is.

AUTHOR'S NOTE: Actor's Equity will provide a list of dinner theaters operating under Equity contracts. See Appendix D for the address.

7

Aramis Estevez

SOMETHING TO BE PROUD OF

Nat Bucknell, the director, had said he would call. "The ones we cast will get a call this evening. The rest of you—well, thank you for auditioning." There had been about fifty kids at the final callback, culled from over three hundred who attended the first audition. Only eight would be used.

Aramis Estevez, thirteen years old at the time, looked at the telephone—again. Then he looked at the clock. Time was running out. He had worked with the director before and thought of him as a friend. Maybe he would call anyway, just to say he was sorry he couldn't use Aramis. After all, the dance part of the audition had not gone well. But he had sung well. And he knew his acting was good. Aramis had been waiting all evening.

The telephone rang. It was for his brother, eight years older. Aramis tried not to look anxious while his brother talked. He tried to be polite, always. That was how their mother had raised them. Good manners, respect, politeness—these things still counted no matter where you were or who you were with. Fortunately his brother was polite too. He sensed that Aramis wanted the line clear, so he quickly finished his call. But the

At age nine Aramis had his first "head shot" taken. This was not long after he met Jeanne Niederlitz, the agent who manages him today. (Photo courtesy of Acting by Children Productions, Inc.)

phone rang again and Aramis tensed when his brother held out the receiver and said, "It's for you."

The call was from a friend asking, "Did he call yet?" The answer was, "No." Aramis ended the conversation quickly. The friend understood. He was an actor too.

This was one of the things about the business that Aramis didn't like. He had made the mistake of really wanting the job. Now, because he had an emotional investment in it, he was paying with anxiety while the clock ran out. Most jobs he could audition for and then go on about his business, not really concerned about whether he got them or not. He had gotten plenty—he would get plenty more, he told himself. He was particularly objective about commercials. They were very hard work, requiring twelve-hour days for a thirty-second spot. Most of the time was spent waiting around for the technicians. Then suddenly they would call the "talent," as actors are called on commercial sets, and expect them to be bright and energetic after sitting quietly in a corner for two hours. The pay was very good, but they weren't much fun. Many times Aramis did not know what the whole commercial would be like until he saw it on television. It's hard to get emotionally involved in work like that. But this job was different.

Dancing with Kings was a celebration of the two hundredth anniversary of Dutch-American diplomatic recognition. It would rehearse in New York and then move to Amsterdam, Holland, where it would perform live for a couple of months and be recorded for television. Aramis knew many of the people involved in the show. If he got the job, he would get to travel to Europe and meet and perform for new people and he would be paid well for the work. If only Nat would call.

"Let's go down to the corner and get some doughnuts." Aramis's mother was standing in the doorway. She didn't often suggest going out. When Aramis was six he was helping her move a piece of furniture when she suddenly grabbed her back and cried out in pain. She had injured her spinal cord and has been disabled ever since. She has good days and bad days. If she was willing to get her cane and suggest they go for an outing, she must be feeling good. Aramis hated to disappoint her. Still . . .

He looked again at the phone. "It's nearly ten o'clock," she said gently with the understanding and compassion that have kept mother and son close. "If he was going to call, he would have done it by now, don't you think?"

With a sigh Aramis resigned himself to the loss of the job. He got up to go. It wasn't easy to think of going back to commercial calls that he didn't like instead of going to rehearsals for a stage show that he did like. But one of the first things Aramis had learned was to be realistic. Hopeful, yes. Optimistic, yes. But realistic.

Moving with his mother could be a slow process. They had almost gotten to the door when the phone

The Mask Maker *was a production of* Acting by Children, *Inc., the same company that produced* Dancing with Kings. *The company produces original musicals with youngsters from disadvantaged neighborhoods. (Photo courtesy of Acting by Children Productions, Inc.)*

rang. Aramis froze. "Well, go answer it," said his mother with a giggle in her voice. She listened and nodded as Aramis told Nat that yes he wanted to do the show and yes he would come in to sign the contract and yes he would get a passport. Aramis was thrilled. So was his mother.

It was his mother who got the whole thing started. The poverty all around their Brooklyn apartment was oppressive. Aspirations among the young were limited to dead-end jobs like pushing hamburgers at McDonald's and "the streets." "The streets" could mean an unbroken cycle of public assistance or crime or drugs or all three. Rosa Estevez was determined her boys would do better than that. She hadn't come to America from Dominica in the Caribbean just to sink into the same poverty and waste she had escaped.

When she had seen an announcement of a summer theater program at a nearby playground, she had encouraged Aramis to go. At first he had hesitated. He wasn't interested in singing and dancing. He had his nine-year-old sights set on engineering. He didn't know anything about show business. There were many reasons not to go. But Rosa persisted and, to please her, Aramis went to the playground. He did everything he could to please her. Since the accident three years before, she had been through so much pain. There had been the operations and the doctors and the medicines. There had been the days when she couldn't even get out of bed. There had been the look of discomfort on her face even when she could get up. If she really wanted him to go to this playground theater, he would go.

The director of the program was Jeanne Neiderlitz. When Aramis joined them, she saw something special almost immediately. The bold, regular features, the honey-colored complexion, and the neatly groomed curly hair were only part of the overall package. Whether from having to accept more responsibility than a youngster should because of his mother's disability, or simply from a native gift, the boy was intelligent. Not just bright. Not just mature beyond his years. There was a very active mind at work here, and it showed itself in good manners, attentive listening, and focused concentration. The busy intellect guided the attractive body through a learning process that quickly turned the boy who wanted to be an engineer into a boy who wanted to be an actor.

Jeanne manages young talent, and she started sending Aramis out on professional calls. The results have been impressive. Today at fifteen Aramis lists thirty commercials and over one hundred fifty voice-overs on his résumé. He has appeared on *Sesame Street* with Mary Tyler Moore and has played roles on *One Life to Live, Search for Tomorrow,* and *As the World Turns.* He has done three feature films, including *Fort Apache The Bronx* with Paul Newman. He has traveled to Connecticut, California, and New Hampshire to appear in plays, and he has been in several off-Broadway productions. He is currently in the Broadway production of *Big River,* a musical adaptation of Mark Twain's *Huckleberry Finn.* The show won seven Tony awards, including best musical of the year. The résumé would be impressive for an actor twice Aramis's age.

Relaxing in the dimly lit audience seats of the Eugene O'Neill theater on a recent July afternoon, Aramis warms quickly to an interview. His rich, well-modulated voice is clear, and his look is casual but neat. Dressed in white shorts and a turquoise top, he seems very much at home in the theater and smiles as Rene Auberjonois (best known as the finicky politician from the *Benson* TV series) and other cast members drift through and wave on their way to prepare for the Wednesday matinee performance of *Big River.* The harsh whiteness of the work lights is in sharp contrast to the warm earth colors of the set. Somewhere a guitar player slowly warms up his instrument and his fingers.

"My very first audition was for a movie with Richard Pryor and Cicely Tyson," Aramis said. "It went well and I got to the final callback. The thing was, I had been assigned a guardian for the day who took me to the wrong place. And that was the final day of casting, so I missed out completely."

The press agent for *Big River* who arranged the interview stops by to make sure both actor and interviewer have everything they need. Satisfied the meeting is going well, he hurries off with briefcase in hand.

Aramis begins to talk about his three-month engagement as a host on *Wonderama*. "The audition was weird. I went in and everybody was there. There was a whole crowd of people and everyone was busy. I didn't think anyone was listening to me. They told me to just look in the camera and talk about myself for at least five minutes. So I just got into my whole life story. They called up about a week later and told me I got the job."

When asked about really wanting a particular role, he tells of the Broadway production of *Peter Pan* with Sandy Duncan. "I had gone to at least ten callbacks for that. At the final callback it was between me and this other guy, and we auditioned our hearts out. I never put so much into an audition. Then I stayed up the whole night thinking about it. Then, the next day, my manager called them and they said that they were going to hire both of us. But the stage manager had a son that she wanted in the show." It's a familiar story to most actors. You think you have a job and then someone comes out of the woodwork and takes the job away.

His first commercial was for a *Star Wars* toy. Luckily, in addition to being an athlete, in his spare time Aramis is a *Star Wars* buff. He says he's learned "everything" about *Star Wars* and that knowledge and enthusiam helped him get the commercial. While talking about sports and *Star Wars* and his own guitar, another color

At fifteen Aramis Estevez is a handsome young man with a solid professional background and a bright theatrical future.

in the personality of this colorful young man becomes obvious to the interviewer. Not only is he a practiced professional performer, he is also a kid with hobbies and energy and a fun side like any other kid. When asked for his best quality, he hesitates before saying, "Respect. I treat my friends and people I meet with respect and friendliness. I think that's important." When asked for his worst qualities, he smiles and admits to occasional moodiness and a bad temper which he tries hard to control.

He talks briefly about Professional Children's School, where he is enrolled. It has a flexible program that covers every subject taught in a nonprofessional school. But at PCS classes begin at 10:00 A.M. and rotate daily so that a performer who may have been at the theater until nearly midnight the night before will miss only one session of an early biology class if he gets to school late one morning. When students are touring or in final rehearsals for a show, lesson plans are prepared and much of their work is done by correspondence. Attractive as that seems, it also requires a great deal of discipline on the part of the student.

Aramis dates occasionally and used to have a steady girlfriend. But recently he has been trying to meet a variety of young ladies. With the professional wages he has made, he could probably conduct a more elaborate social life. But his mother has established a trust fund for his money and most of his day-to-day living expenses come out of the family income. When he is eighteen he will have access to most of what he has made in his young but active career.

His mother has done a lot for him. Aramis calls her his best friend and speaks warmly of someday supporting her and trying to repay her faith in him. "I'm proud of my work and I'm proud of my Hispanic heritage," he says. "But mostly I want her to be proud of me."

Several actors settle in nearby seats and chat with growing animation as curtain time draws near and the performance energy begins to build. A sound technician tests the speakers with a series of bird calls used in the show. Dan Jenkins, who plays Huck Finn, searches through a gym bag for a book he wants to show another actor. An unseen piano joins the unseen guitar. The interviewer senses an involuntary shift in Aramis from casual talk to professional responsibility. The interview is drawing to a close.

"She's been through so much," says Aramis, returning the discussion to his mother. "That's one reason I'm doing all this—to give her something to be proud of."

Clearly she can be very proud of this young man with proven talent and clear vision who has made a place for himself in the front ranks of professional theater.

AUTHOR'S NOTE: The Sunday *New York Times* carries the most up-to-date listings of theater and dance activities on and off Broadway. Most libraries keep it among their periodicals.

Appendix A

WHAT IS "PROFESSIONAL"?

There are many types of theater in America today. Generally they fall into one of four categories:

Community theater includes "little" theaters, club and recreation theaters, and theaters sponsored by religious groups. The unifying element in these is that the performers are not paid. Some groups have paid technical and management staffs and large budgets, and some even bring in an occasional paid guest performer. As a rule, however, the actors on the stage are there for the love of performing or for the fun and fellowship of the theater experience.

Educational theaters, like community theaters, use unpaid performers. Those performers, however, are usually students of the school or college sponsoring the performance, and the productions are designed to give them experience in front of an audience and exposure to a broad range of theater styles. This will enhance both their general education and their future professional expertise.

Semi-professional theaters pay some or all of their actors. However, the rate of pay and the general working conditions are not up to the standards set by the prevailing unions in the industry. The artistic merit of these companies may be very high, but it is important to understand that they are not classified with similar companies operating under union jurisdiction. Semi-professional theaters include many summer stock companies that draw their talent from vacationing college students and teachers. There are a number of semi-professional dinner theaters and children's theaters as well.

Professional theaters are those that are recognized by the prevailing theater unions, agree to abide by work rules established by the unions, and pay according to the appropriate union scale. Actors' Equity Association is the union that represents the thirty-five thousand professional actors in America.

In addition to being an art, acting is also a trade. Professional actors try to make their living from the acting trade. Most start out working in community or semi-professional theaters. Eventually they must join the union in order to work in theaters that pay more and offer better working conditions. Once they join the union they are no longer allowed to work in any nonprofessional theater.

There is an old joke that makes the rounds of theater people:

Question: How do you get into a union show?
Answer: First you have to belong to Actors' Equity.
Question: How do you join Actors' Equity?
Answer: First you have to have a job in a union show.

In fact, it is not quite that closed today. Currently there is a policy whereby young people can earn credits toward their union membership through a "membership candidate" program. These credits come from working in productions in which the union allows a limited number of nonunion actors. In some large cast shows in theaters outside New York there are several small roles—"spear carriers" they are sometimes called—that can be played by "nonpros," meaning nonunion actors. After completing fifty weeks working in such roles, the beginner may apply to the union for membership.

Some beginning actors have worked out arrangements with producers of dinner theater or summer stock companies so that they will work for a set number of weeks as a "nonpro" at a reduced salary if the producer will sign them to an Equity contract after that time. Once an actor has been offered a union contract, admission to the union is automatic.

In some cases a commercial producer will offer a contract to an actor on the basis of either outstanding talent or an outstanding skill or look. If a producer needs someone who can juggle and sing at the same time, and the only person available is not a union member, the producer may offer that person a contract, and that person must then join the union. In the same way, a producer casting a small child is not necessarily interested in whether the child is already a member of the union. If the child has the look and the talent the producer is looking for, he or she is offered a contract and joins the union on that basis.

Once the young actor has joined the union, he or she is protected by working conditions established by Actors' Equity. He or she is also subject to the minimum salaries established for the type of contract offered. On Broadway the minimum currently is $700 per week.

Stars may have negotiated several thousand per week, but no actor, including children, can be paid less than the minimum. Off-Broadway scale runs from $225 to $435 depending on the size of the house. Regional theaters, including summer stock and repertory companies, range from $306 to $394 per week, again depending on the size of the house and the potential gross receipts from ticket sales. The lowest paid contract is the Theater for Young Audiences agreement used for touring school shows. The performers working in these shows are paid $220 per week (1985-86 season figures).

In addition to salary, producers pay a per diem for each day a touring actor is away from the home city. (They also pay all transportation costs for touring and for bringing an actor from his or her home city to the theater location.) This money is for hotel and meal expenses.

The word *amateur* literally means "one who loves his work." Amateurs are those who do the work because they love it. They are careful with the details of their work habits, they try to improve their technique, and they constantly continue to read and study and expand their understanding of the thing they love. They devote time and energy, thought and care to their "profession." If it can be said that anyone who is paid is a professional, it can also be said that while an amateur is not a professional, a good professional is always a good amateur.

Appendix B

WHAT THE GROWN-UPS SAY—Two Viewpoints

Christopher Parsons, artistic director of the Naples (Florida) Dinner Theater, was the first to recognize Jessica Long as a potential professional talent. For nearly twenty years Parsons has been directing children in both noncommercial theaters and in the more economically demanding arena of professional dinner theater. The popularity of child performers on Florida stages has made him something of an expert on young actors. He has seen dozens over the years and he has also watched his two sons grow up around the theaters in which he has worked.

"The most important thing is a 'sparkle,' " says Parsons. "I don't know any better way to describe it. There is that little something extra that makes this kid want to be seen—that makes that kid special. A little bit of spark that makes them *interesting*."

Yet there is more than talent and personality involved. "The other thing that is just as crucial to me is a businesslike attitude. I don't mind if they want to have fun and play. That's what I'm selling. I don't want little adults. But I need them to focus. I get turned off at an audition by a kid who can't keep focused on what we're doing."

Parsons says that the ability to focus usually shows up during dance auditions. His wife choreographs most of his productions, and he watches carefully while she works. If a kid can pay attention during the very physical dance activity, then there's a chance that the ability to concentrate will translate itself into other areas of rehearsal. For that reason he usually has his wife take children auditionees through a dance routine even if the play is a nonmusical.

Parsons also wants to be sure that the parents of a child actor support what the child is doing. But he draws the line at the stage door. "If I find parents pushy—if they want to become involved critically at every step of the way—it usually turns me off. I had one little girl who was brilliant, but I stopped using her after one show because the mother was such a pain to work with. It's a shame. But I can't help her. That's *her* mother. She was born that way."

Anne Steel is a professional agent in New York. Since most professional children enter the business with little or no experience, the agent or manager can be crucial in career development. As the person who knows both how the business *should* work and how it really *does* work, the agent can be the bridge between the parent/child party and the production company.

When she is looking at new talent, Anne is very clear about what she wants. "Intelligence," she says, "literally, IQ. Intelligence and parents who can support the kid's efforts."

When asked about the charge that young people in show business are often exposed to "too much too soon," Anne clearly comes down on the side of the profession. "For an intelligent child with a support system of decent adult human beings, it's an enormous asset to have the experience. They [the child actors] can develop tremendous insights. They are far more well-rounded than kids from a 'normal' public school environment. I doubt seriously that anything they see is any more sordid, and it's in a positive creative environment.

"There is a real structure [in a theatrical production] and there is no place that I can think of where such self-discipline is required as for a kid to be on Broadway."

When asked what advice she would give to kids in middle America who think they may want to go into theater, she is equally clear. "Get out of middle America and go do it. And the younger the better. Twenty-two is too late."

Appendix C
THE CASTING NOTICE

The following casting notice was posted at Actors' Equity and printed in the trade paper *Back Stage* during the summer of 1985. It is typical of dozens of notices that appear each week. In addition to learning the obvious facts presented here, the experienced professional can learn a great deal from this notice that is not specifically spelled out. This ability to analyze information—to "read between the lines"—is important both in preparing for auditions and in deciding which auditions to go to.

EQ., "SHORT CHANGED"

7/16 from 10 AM-1 & 2-6 PM at AEA Audition Center, 165 W. 46 St., 2nd fl.

Producer Fred Kolo will hold auditions for "Short Change" at AEA Audition Center, 165 W. 46 St. Mini-contract. Dir.: Joshua Astrachan; author: Geoffrey Gordon. *Breakdown*—**Benjamin**: 21, native New Yorker, aspiring writer, athletic, intellectual, romantic, intense; **Daniel**: 18, actor from Long Island, innocent, attractive, good-hearted, self-centered, skillful deadpan comedian, understudy only; **Fred**: 21, the prime behind-the-scenes mover on campus, humorous, manic, wiry, witty and chic, understudy only; **Rayna**: female, 23, music major, good-looking, charming, trying to live a normal life in the face of an uncertain future, understudy only. Bring light contemporary monologue, two min. or less.

Tues. July 16—Eq. actors, 10-1, 2-6 PM.

(Reprinted by permission of
Back Stage Publications)

Experienced professionals would look carefully at the names of everyone involved to see if there is someone with whom they have worked before. They would also check their memory for other actors they know who have worked with these people and check out the style, personality, and taste of those in charge. If an actor reading this remembers that a friend once worked with Fred Kolo, he might call to find out more about Mr. Kolo before going to an audition. Personality plays an important role in casting.

Further, the reader can tell that since this is a "mini" contract, the pay will be little and the theater will be one of the smaller of the off-Broadway houses. It will most likely be set up for a short run with the vague possibility of moving to a larger house if the reviews are good and additional investors can be found. For some actors this information may be important since they may or may not be willing to take a chance on this kind of risky production if they have other, more lucrative opportunities.

The fact that three of the four roles are listed as "understudy only" means that the show is essentially already cast. It may have been done in showcase or it may be a group of friends. Whatever the case, unless the actor is right for the role of Benjamin, there is little chance of getting a performing role.

Finally, from the description of the characters it is clear that there is a college setting, there is a lot of humor, and since there is only the one girl, there will probably be some form of romance. The experienced reader would classify this as a light comedy that takes place in a college setting and would dress for the audition to reflect that aspect of his or her personality. Clearly a three-piece suit or a tailored dress is wrong for this interview. Clearly Shakespeare or Ibsen, no matter how well you do it, is wrong for this audition piece. The alert performer would dress casually and prepare a piece of Neil Simon or some other "light" writer for this audition.

Appendix D

RESOURCES

UNIONS

Actors' Equity Association
165 West 46 Street
New York, N.Y. 10036
(Actors' Equity will provide lists of current stock, dinner theater, and LORT [repertory] theaters on request.)

American Federation of Television and Radio Artists
1350 Avenue of the Americas, 2nd Floor
New York, N.Y. 10019
(AFTRA represents actors involved in radio and live television.)

Screen Actors Guild
1700 Broadway
New York, N.Y. 10019
(SAG represents actors working on film for both movies and TV.)

Society of Stage Directors and Choreographers, Inc.
1501 Broadway
New York, N.Y. 10036

SERVICE ORGANIZATIONS

American Theater Association
1010 Wisconsin Avenue NW
Washington, D.C. 20007
(ATA is a service organization for all kinds of theater,
including professional, educational, and community. Its
annual *Directory* includes theater addresses and directors' names from all over the country and can be found
in many libraries.)

Theatre Communications Group, Inc.
355 Lexington Avenue
New York, N.Y. 10017
(TCG is a service organization for not-for-profit regional
theaters. Their annual *Theatre Profiles* gives up-to-date
information on the regional theater field and can be
found in many libraries. It also publishes an extensive
list of books and pamphlets on various theater issues
and will send a list on request.)

The Dramatists Guild
234 West 44 Street
New York, N.Y. 10036
(DG is the functioning union for playwrights. Each year
it sponsors a Young Playwrights Contest and co-pro-
duces a number of winning entries in New York. Write
for further information.)

Foundation for the Extension and Development of the
American Professional Theatre
165 West 46 Street
New York, N.Y. 10036
(FEDAPT publishes a number of valuable booklets on
theater development. The foundation will provide a
publications list on request.)

The New York Arts Group
P.O. Box 489
Old Chelsea Station
New York, N.Y. 10011
(NYAG is a fellowship of Christian artists, who meet on a regular basis and issue a periodic newsletter. Write for further information.)

Institute of Outdoor Drama
The University of North Carolina at Chapel Hill
202 Graham Memorial 052 A
Chapel Hill, N.C. 27514
(IOD is the service organization for outdoor dramas. Send postage to receive a current list of companies. In addition they publish a newsletter. Write for further information.)

Most of the organizations listed have newsletters that can be subscribed to by nonmembers. Fees vary, so write for a current schedule.

In addition some of the groups listed (in particular ATA) offer inexpensive memberships for students. Serious theater students may wish to explore membership as a way of keeping informed about national theater activities.

SCHOOLS

Many colleges have distinguished theater departments and cannot be faulted for both the seriousness of their program and the success of their alumni. Some small schools have individual teachers who are as gifted as the most well-known university scholars. Ultimately the decision on where to train must come from a variety of factors, including family finances, entrance requirements, and the type of degree desired.

The following schools have a unique bond in that they have designed their programs to meet the needs of "professional" theater training. That is, they have geared their courses to address students who intend to make a living from full-time theater work, and they have banded together into an organization called the League of Professional Theatre Training Programs.

American Conservatory Theatre
Professional Theatre Training Programs
450 Geary Street
San Francisco, Calif. 94102

Boston University
James V. Nicholson, Coordinator of Admissions
School of Theatre Arts, Room 472
855 Commonwealth Avenue
Boston, Mass. 02215

Carnegie-Mellon University
Office of Admissions
5000 Forbes Avenue
Pittsburgh, Pa. 15213

The Juilliard School
Office of Admissions
Lincoln Center
New York, N.Y. 10023

New York University
Tisch School of the Arts
Theatre Program
725 Broadway, Fifth Floor
New York, N.Y. 10003

North Carolina School of the Arts
Director of Admissions
200 Waughtown Street
Winston-Salem, N.C. 27107

Theatre SMU
Southern Methodist University
Dallas, Texas 75275

Theater Arts and Film Division
State University of New York
College at Purchase
Purchase, N.Y. 10577

Department of Theater
Temple University
Philadelphia, Pa. 19122

University of California, San Diego
Master of Fine Arts Program
Department of Drama BO44
La Jolla, Calif. 92093

University of Washington
School of Drama BH-20
Seattle, Wash. 98195

Yale School of Drama
Yale University 1903-A
New Haven, Conn. 06520

Each of these schools publishes its own catalogue. For a brochure giving a brief description of each program write:

The League of Professional Theatre Training Programs
1860 Broadway
Suite 1515
New York, N.Y. 10023

Glossary

AGENT An agent represents actors by submitting them for consideration for parts, negotiating *contracts* and sorting out conflicts between jobs. Agents are franchised by the unions and take a ten percent commission for their work. See *manager*.

AFTRA The American Federation of Television and Radio Artists is the actor's union that oversees all live and videotaped broadcasting. See *SAG, EQUITY*.

APPRENTICE An apprentice is a nonunion member of an *Equity* company. Apprentices, sometimes called interns, help out backstage, build scenery and *costumes*, usher, and sometimes play small roles.

ASM An assistant stage manager helps the *stage manager* run the backstage operation, calls actors to the stage, runs errands, cues technicians, etc. The job is sometimes taken by an actor in the show.

AUDITION A screening process by which the *director* interviews actors for roles. Sometimes the actor prepares a short piece of his or her own choosing. Sometimes he or she is asked to read from the script. A *director* may audition dozens of actors for each role. See *casting director*.

BACKER   A backer is anyone who invests money in a production. Each commercial production is set up as an independent corporation, and the backers, sometimes called "angels" are the stockholders.

BILLING   Billing is the relative rank an actor's name is given in advertising. "Star billing" means the actor's name appears immediately before or immediately after the title of the play. "Second billing" means the actor's name appears immediately after the star, etc.

CALL   Call refers to any appointment at a specific time. There are *rehearsal* calls, *costume* calls for fittings, photo calls for picture-taking, etc.

CALLBACK   A callback means that the *director* has seen a large number of actors for a role and has "called back" a few to *audition* again. See *audition, casting director*.

CALL BOARD   The call board is the official bulletin board where schedules, information, *notices,* messages, etc. are posted.

CARD   A union membership card is used to identify union members at *auditions* and union events. In New York some merchants will give discounts on goods and services upon presentation of a union card.

CASTING DIRECTOR   A casting director is hired by the *director* to screen actors in early *auditions.* When a show is casting, there may be several hundred actors considered. The casting director narrows these down to just a few candidates for each role who are then *called back* to *audition* for the *director.*

CHOREOGRAPHER Dances and complex movement sequences like fight scenes are designed by a choreographer.

CHORUS In a musical the actors and actresses who sing and dance in groups are the chorus. If a performer speaks lines or does a solo number, he or she becomes a "principal."

CLASS Many actors and actresses continue to take classes in acting, dance, and voice while they are working professionally.

CONTRACT A contract is a legal document that states the terms of employment. *Equity* contracts state the actor's name, role, play title, date of first *rehearsal,* opening date, and salary. Contracts also include all the standard work rules and any other provisions either the *producer* or the actor negotiates. See *Rider.*

CONVERSION When a production moves from one size theater to another (i.e., off-Broadway to Broadway) it converts to the new contract rules for that theater.

COSTUMES Anything an actor wears onstage is considered a costume, whether it is a period garment or a T-shirt and jeans.

DANCE CAPTAIN The dance captain is the dancer selected by the *choreographer* to keep the dances running smoothly when the *choreographer* is not there.

DEPUTY Each cast elects a deputy to represent the other actors in problems involving union regulations. A deputy must see that both actors and *management* are living up to the rules.

DIRECTOR The director is the person who plans what goes on the stage. He or she designs movement patterns for the actors, helps them with playing scenes, tells the designers what style costumes and scenery to build, and sets the cues for lights and sound effects.

DRESS Dress is slang for "dress rehearsal," at which costumes and makeup and technical effects are tried out.

DUES Dues are payments to the union by the actor. Equity dues are currently two percent of an actor's salary.

EQUITY Actors' Equity Association. See Appendix A.

EPA, EPI Equity principal auditions or Equity principal interviews. See *open call*.

GENERAL MANAGER A general manager works for the *producer* and runs the business of the production, pays bills, writes salary checks, keeps records, etc.

HALF HOUR Half hour is a *call* thirty minutes before curtain time. All actors are supposed to be in the theater by half hour.

INITIATION FEE A payment to the union at the time the actor joins is called an initiation fee. The current *Equity* fee is $500.

INGENUE   A young woman with a romantic look and personality is called an ingenue. The term can refer to either a character or an actress.

JUVENILE   A young man with an immature look is called a juvenile. As with an *ingenue,* the term can mean either the actor or the character.

LEAD   The term means either the most prominent character in the play (played by a *star* in a commercial production) or the leading actor in a particular company.

MANAGEMENT   The owners and operators of a production or a theater company are known collectively as management. This is a union term and is meant to define the difference between the people who perform or provide a service (actors, stagehands, *directors,* designers, etc.) and those who hire them (*producers,* general *managers, casting directors,* etc.)

MANAGER   In addition to an *agent,* an actor may employ a manager to advise on career development. Managers are more personally and directly involved with actors and take a fifteen to twenty percent commission on the actor's salary.

MATINEE   An afternoon performance is called a matinee.

MINIMUM   A minimum is the lowest salary the union will allow a member to be paid in a particular theater. See Appendix A.

MUSICAL DIRECTOR   A musical director teaches the actors their songs, sets the speed and timing of the music, and usually conducts the orchestra.

NOTICE A *producer* closes a production by posting an announcement on the *call board* that the company will stop performing on a certain date. This date must be announced no less than two weeks before the closing. The announcement is called a closing notice or simply notice.

OPEN CALL An open call is an *audition*/interview at which a *director, casting director,* or their representative must see any union member who shows up. Each commercial production must hold an open call (see EPA/EPI), and hundreds of actors usually appear. These are sometimes called "cattle calls" because so many actors are crowded together in a small area, they seem like cattle in a pen.

PER DIEM In addition to salary, a *producer* must pay each actor a set amount for living expenses for each day the actor is away from home on tour or *tryout.*

PIX/PIC 8″ by 10″ glossy photographs of the actor's face are sometimes requested by mail from *directors.* In print they are called pix, as an abbreviation for pictures.

PRESS AGENT The person who helps advertise a production by setting up interviews for newspaper, television, and radio reporters, sends photographs and announcements to the media, and keeps track of stories that are being written about a production is called a press agent.

PREVIEW Many productions give several public or private performances before the official opening of a show so that actors and *directors* can see how the show works in front of an audience and make changes, if necessary, before the critics see the production on opening night. See *tryout.*

PRODUCER   A producer does all the business of the production. He or she makes arrangements with the writer to do the script, rents a theater, arranges for *backers* to finance the show, hires the *director,* and helps put together the production team.

READ   An *audition* sometimes includes reading from a new script. Actors frequently refer to "reading for a role."

READING   In order to hear how dialogue sounds, or to attract *backers,* a *producer* will sometimes arrange for a group of actors to simply sit at a table and read the script. This is called a reading.

REHEARSAL   The work sessions at which the actors and *director* arrange movement (blocking) and practice performing the play are called rehearsals. Sometimes rehearsals involve only a short scene or musical number. Sometimes rehearsals are run-throughs of whole acts or a whole play.

RÉSUMÉ   A résumé lists an actor's name, address, phone number, and physical description. It also lists an actor's previous experience in the theater and/or in films and television. Résumés are usually attached to the back of the actor's picture. See *pix/pic.*

RIDER   Special *contract* provisions are called riders and are typed on separate sheets attached to a standard *contract* form. Riders may refer to *billing,* dressing room conditions, traveling conditions, or any other matter. Young actors usually travel with a parent, and a rider may spell out that the *producer* will pay for the parent's transportation and a *per diem.*

ROOM AND BOARD   If an out-of-town theater has living quarters for actors and staff, as many summer

112

stock and dinner theaters do, a *rider* may make an actor's accommodations and meals a part of the *contract*. This is called room and board.

SAFE AND SANITARY   This is a set of rules that guarantees that the *producer* will provide rest rooms, clean dressing rooms, safe surfaces to dance on, and other conditions that protect the work environment.

SERVICE   Many actors employ an answering service to take messages for them when they are away from their home telephone.

SAG   The Screen Actors Guild is the union that has jurisdiction over all work done on film, whether for movies or for television. Most actors belong to Equity, AFTRA, and SAG.

SHOWCASE   Under certain conditions, the union will allow new plays to be done under the "showcase code." Actors can work in these productions, sometimes called off-off-Broadway, for little or no money. However, they then have a claim on future money the script may make. Showcases have very limited runs in very small theaters and are an advantage to both writers who want to try out new material and to performers, who can invite *agents* to see their work.

SIGN-IN   By *half-hour* every actor must have signed in on a sheet posted on the *call board*. The *stage manager* then checks to see if anyone is missing and if *understudies* must be called.

STAGE MANAGER   During *rehearsals* the SM, or stage manager, is the primary assistant to the *director*. He or she takes notes on blocking (movement), posts calls and official information, sets cues for lights and sound, etc. During performance the SM runs the back-

113

stage area, calling actors to the stage and cueing the technicians who run the various stage effects.

STAR   A star is anyone whose name is likely to attract people to the theater.

STRIKE   To strike is to remove something. A prop may be struck or an entire set may be removed from the stage or from the theater. A *director* may say "Strike the candles from that table," meaning take the candles away. A *stage manager* may say "Strike the Act I set and set up for Act II," meaning remove one set and set up another. When a play closes, the entire set is "struck," or removed from the theater.

STOCK   The term stock comes from a time when most plays had a standard set of characters. Touring stock companies were made up of a leading man and leading lady, a young leading couple (see *ingenue* and *juvenile*) and character men and women. In stock companies today, one or two actors will play all the leading parts and other roles will be taken by character people. *Apprentices* may then get to play any parts that are left over.

TECH   *Tech*nical rehearsals are for the people who run the lights and sound and move scenery and props. Actors walk through their movements and say the lines that cue the effects. That way the technicians can see exactly how long they have to run their various cues.

THEATRE   Most people involved in theater spell the word with an "r-e" ending instead of the American standard "e-r." This is out of respect for the Greek origin of the term *theatron,* which was first translated as "theatre."

TITLE CHARACTER   Sometimes a character is mentioned in the title of a play. *The Diary of Anne Frank* is such a play, and the actress playing Anne is said to be playing the title character.

TKTS   In Times Square in New York there is a booth operated by the Theater Development Fund which sells theater tickets at half price on the day of performance. This booth is known as the TKTS booth.

TRADES   On Wednesday and Thursday of each week several newspapers are issued in New York that have casting news and items about the theater and media trades. These trade papers are usually spoken of as "the trades."

TRYOUT   Before a play opens in New York a *producer* will often set up short runs in cities like Boston, Philadelphia, or Washington so that the piece can be "tried out" in front of audiences. Often changes are made in the play or in scenery or costumes based on these tryout performances. Tryouts are different from *previews,* which take place in New York.

UNDERSTUDY   An understudy learns the part played by another actor and is ready to play that part if the primary actor gets sick or can't perform for any reason. Sometimes actors playing small roles will understudy larger roles. If they have to perform the larger role, a "general understudy" will take their small part. Understudies are different from "alternates," who are hired to play specific performances of particularly difficult roles. Often alternates will play *matinees* and the regular actor will play all the evening shows.

UNEMPLOYMENT Unemployment insurance is provided by the government for people who are temporarily out of work. Since actors are often "between jobs," most of them apply for it at one time or another. Even major stars will sometimes go to unemployment offices and stand in line to sign for their checks.

UPTOWN/DOWNTOWN Most of the Broadway theaters are located around Times Square in New York. This is considered "uptown," since most of the off-Broadway theaters are in Greenwich Village, which is "downtown." Ironically some off-Broadway theaters are farther uptown than the Broadway theaters. When *Hurlyburly* opened at a theater on Seventy-seventh Street, it was considered off-Broadway. When it moved to a Broadway theater on Forty-seventh Street (downtown), it was reported to be moving "uptown."

Index